AWAKENING

THE CHILD HEART

Handbook for Global Parenting

By Carla Hannaford

Permission for use of the following is gratefully acknowledged:
Brain Gym® is a Registered Trademark of the Educational Kinesiology Foundation.
Illustrations on Figure 1.1, Changing Heart Rhythms is copyright Institute of HeartMath
Figure 2.4, PET Scans after Marcel Reichel, George Washington University
Figure 9.2, photograph by Sally White, Palm Bay, Florida
Figure 9.4, photograph by Cherokee, Shaner, Honaunau, Hawaii.
Figure 10.3, photograph by Susan Kovalik and Associates, Kent, Washington

Cover design and painting by Greg Overton, COPANMEDIA
greoverton@hotmail.com
Copyright © 2002 by Carla Hannaford
Cover artwork copyright © 2002 by Jamilla Nur Publishing
Illustrations (except as indicated above) copyright © 2002 by Carla Hannaford

Jamilla Nur Publishing
P.O. Box 338
Captain Cook, Hawaii 96704
EMAIL: Heartconnect44@cs.com

Library of Congress Cataloging in Publication Data
Hannaford, Carla
Awakening the Child Heart: handbook for global parenting/Carla Hannaford
1st Edition
        P.
            cm.
Includes bibliographical references and index.
ISBN 0-9716647-0-6   (trade pbk.:alk. paper)
    1. Mind and body. 2. Physiology of learning. 3. Play physiology. I. Title
Library of Congress Control Number: 200111985

Printed in the United States of America
10 9 8 7 6 5 4 3 2

"If presently unborn generations are to flourish optimally and create an earth culture of grand and joyous proportions, then their parents should read this book and heed its wonderfully expressive message. I was deeply touched by this book and wish that I could have read it as a young husband before my children were conceived."
—Dr. William A. Tiller, Professor Emeritus, Stanford, University and Author of *Science and Human Transformation and Consciousness* and *Conscious Acts of Creation*.

"Carla Hannaford continues to lead the field in mind/body development with the rhythms of the heart, emotions and play. Her high esteem in intellect, creativity and joy weave the best of teaching skills into practical and necessary nutrition for educators and parents. This book helps update the professionals, educate the novices and inspire everyone that there is a heart to the science of learning."
—Don Campbell, Author of *The Mozart Effect* and *The Mozart Effect for Children*.

"Hannaford's great contribution is not only that she turns years and even centuries of research into techniques to make life easier, but that never for a moment does she let us forget that there is a living, breathing, feeling human being attached to this tangle of nerves and muscles and that this person is somehow greater than all its parts!"
—Svea Gold, Author of *If Kids Just Came with Instruction Sheets!*, and creator of the video *Autism, Neurological Research and Neuro-developmental Therapy*.

"A book like *Awakening the Child Heart* is overdue. For years bits of information from a variety of scholars have been seeping out, signaling some major problems in our changed ways of child-rearing. Dr. Hannaford has pulled these bits together in a compelling synthesis which every parent, potential parent, and educator needs to read. Moreover, this book sparkles with hope for those of us willing to put our children first, which they require and deserve, and to cultivate the child mind in ourselves."

—Dr. Catherine Warrick, former Dean of Education and EEO Director for the State of Minnesota, and present co-owner of The Whole Brain Shop, and Educational Kinesiology center in St. Paul, MN.

"Carla Hannaford has long been in the business of awakening people to essential new and ancient truths. As she teaches us how to go about *Awakening the Child Heart* she opens our eyes and spirits so that we may live more consciously and conscientiously. Follow your heart's desire, follow your strongest intuitions....follow Carla into the realm where spirit and science meld into truth and lead us to the pathway for world healing."

—Chris Brewer, M.A., Musician, Educator and Co-author of *Rhythms of Learning*.

"In this book, Carla Hannaford builds a bridge between some of the latest scientific insights and the best of conscious parenting. The joy in this book is the warmth and heart with which Carla treats her broad scope, making it inviting to read and a treasure for every reader."

—Win and Bill Sweet, Authors of *Living Joyfully with Children*.

*I dedicate this book to the family bond that begins
with my mother, Minnie Foote, my daughter
Breeze and my husband Ahti—
and then extends out to all
the beautiful, coherent people that
bless my life worldwide.*

ACKNOWLEDGEMENTS

A heartfelt thank you to all the following people who were such an inspiration to me as friends and leaders in the field of consciousness, play, music and love: Joseph Chilton Pearce, William and Jean Tiller, Candice Pert and Michael Ruff, Chris Brewer, Don Campbell, Rollin McCraty, Svea Gold, Phyllis Weikert, and Win and Bill Sweet.

A special thanks to Margaret and Mark Esterman for teaching me how to get my thoughts and emotions into writing, and supporting me with the production of this book. And also to Catherine Warrick for her final editing, and Linda Perry for her excellent book layout.

I also wish to acknowledge the following people who have given me their wisdom, time and love in birthing this book: Cheeah and Fairoh, Bonnie Hershey, Willy Welzenbach, Susan Dermond, Johanna Bangeman, James Lindsey, Jenilyn Merten, Kay Allison, Judy Metcalf, Martha Denny and Lloyd Walker, Esta Feedora, Cal Hashimoto, and Aelbert Aehegma.

My love and appreciation especially go to my daughter Breeze, my former husband Jim Hannaford, and my husband Ahti Mohala for their input, patience and support.

Contents

List of Figures

CHAPTER ONE

The Importance of the Child Heart

*"We are not human if we can no longer experience
awe and wonder at the beauty and mystery of life..."*
—Charlene Spretnak.[1]

The image of the child heart fills this book. All the other seemingly disparate topics coalesce to teach us what the child heart is and that many factors conspire to either foster its emergence or suppress its unfolding. The child heart is not a concept that is synonymous with the hearts of the very young, for sadly, many infants, "rug rats" and toddlers exist who have been denied this priceless possession. Conversely, I know many magnificent people in their golden years who possess such a heart in abundance.

Brain researchers tell us that free natural pleasure grows our brain and allows us to unfold our unlimited potential[2,3], but natural pleasure can't exist without an unencumbered child heart. Natural pleasure occurs through play, learning, creativity, human interaction, and reflective time. The fearful, isolated heart has difficulty in just these arenas of life.

As the events of the 21st century already have demonstrated, cultivating the coherent, connected child heart has become a necessity for the welfare of the world. The angry, disconnected hearts among us are driving us nearer to possible oblivion. The terrorists of our world, set on killing thousands of other human beings for the sake of an idea, retaliation, and maintaining an atmosphere of fear, have forced us to acknowledge that great trouble exists in the collective heart and mind of humanity.

Exploring the child heart is both a profound scientific inquiry and a deeply personal journey for many. This dual exploration has been especially true for me as a scientist and the mother of a wisdom child named Breeze. As a scientist, I marvel at the way physicists, biologists, cardiologists, cognitive scientists, sociologists, neuro-scientists, and a host of other scientists and academicians are drawing closer and closer to the mystical insights of 4000 years of wisdom seekers. As a parent, I alternately shudder under a burden of regret for all I didn't know about growing a child and send up sighs of pleasure that miraculously Breeze, and other beautiful young beings, have managed to survive the unwitting muddling of their well-intentioned parents.

Consequently, this exploration of the child heart runs on two tracks through each phase of its unfolding. Scientific evidence exists for a radical shift in our understanding of what allows all humans to prosper physically, emotionally, intellectually, and spiritually. However, data can be quite dry though intellectually compelling and it feels both emotionally and intellectually inconsistent to discuss the child heart from a scientific point of view only. Fortunately, I enjoy support from my family to use our collective and individual struggles to illustrate how lack of knowledge about the child heart, as well as experiences that have nurtured the child heart in each of us, has altered our lives. I have further support for blending scientific data with a personal story from David Chalmers, a science of consciousness researcher. He believes the reintegration of "third person" information with "first person" experience to be one of the greatest challenges facing science today.[4] I trust this exploration will help, in some small way, to heal the brain-heart split in our global community, and elicit coherence for the sake of this glorious planet we all share.

Inviting Coherence

I remember my childhood as full of magic—warm, fluid summer days, dripping into one another with sweet smells and constant wonder as I nestled in the sensuous, fully leafed branches of a quiet tree or played elaborate imaginative games with the neighborhood kids. So present in the moment was I that only the prolonged shrill whistle of my father brought me back home in the evening. My life was secure in the embrace of a neighborhood community, surrounded by guardians who knew how precious each child was. Even the first few years of school in the early 50's were an extension of my play and a cornucopia of natural pleasures.

It wasn't until the 3rd grade that multiplication tables and my inability to read made me question my invincibility and joy. Then with adolescence came alienation from my father and an eroding sense of trust in my self. I was experiencing the difference between coherence and incoherence, and each shaped my confidence to be creative and authentic, to live and learn with pleasure and passion.

Coherence is a touchstone term throughout this book. The dictionary defines coherence as:

logical connection, consistency, and congruity, the act or fact of holding together as with cohesion, harmonious connection of the parts of a discourse.[5]

In the broad sense, coherence simply means an ordered, consistent, harmonious functioning within any system as with the physical and biochemical systems of our bodies which influence our mental, emotional, physical and spiritual state each moment. For the thesis of this book, coherence also applies to a *conscious pleasure state of being in alignment with our purpose, joy, happiness and connection to others.*

I first became interested in the idea of "coherence" at the International Consciousness Conference in Tucson, Arizona, April 1994. Coherence was being used in reference to an electromagnetic field reading of the heart called a heart rate variability (HRV) pattern. Researchers observed a coherent HRV when a person experienced feelings of appreciation or a playful, harmonious environment, was engrossed in joyful work or learning or meditated. These findings further showed that a coherent heart pattern determined the brain's ability to optimally receive sensory information from the environment. This coherent pattern affected the brain's ability to assimilate and construct understandable patterns from that sensory information, remember them, learn from them and act on them in appropriate, effective, and creative ways.

When stressed or frustrated, the heart rate variability pattern was shown to become incoherent, causing incoherent patterns in the brain. These incoherent patterns decreased the brain's ability to take in sensory information, make an understandable pattern of it, and act on it appropriately. The ability to learn (beyond simple survival) is greatly reduced during an incoherent state.[6]

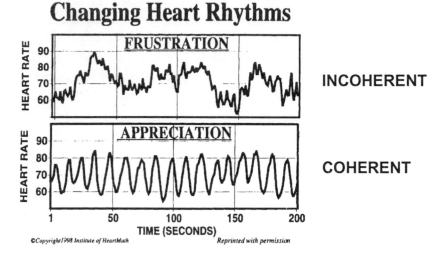

Figure 1.1: *Changing Heart Rhythms*
from the HeartMath Institute's Research

One wave of electrical current across the heart between the atria and ventricals is designated the Q,R,S,T wave on an electrocardiogram (EKG/ECG).

By measuring the beat-to-beat variation in R-R intervals, we can obtain the Heart Rate Variability (HRV) pattern which gives us important physiological parameters of heart rate changes over time and dynamically reflects our inner emotional state and stress levels.[7,8,9]

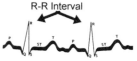

Figure 1.2: *Electrocardiogram (EKG or ECG)*

Vibrational Coherence

According to quantum physics, all matter is energy existing as vibration; therefore, we as humans are, in essence, vibration existing in a sea of vibration. Coherence is an integral part of that vibrational world—with all vibrations either being coherent or incoherent. Throughout our bodies we have finely tuned receptors that transform these vibrations into the touchable, see-able, hear-able sensations we think of as matter and the physical world.

Learning and memory are based on our ability to make coherent patterns from sensory information. In order for us to develop a visual image, our mind/body system must put together intricate patterns of space, weight, texture, form and color from the vibrational sensations we receive. Likewise, learning the complex patterns of language begins in utero and is optimized by coherence within the system. *The coherence of the brain is determined by the coherence of the heart.*

The vibrations we sensorily depend on most are sound and visible light waves. These are either harmonious, congruent, consistent and, therefore, coherent with the natural vibrational milieu of our cells, tissues, organs and entire body, or they are not. Coherent sound and music tends to align with the body's own coherent vibrations making it easy and energizing to listen to, not discordant or agitating.

Light and sound waves can be scattered and incongruent and, therefore, incoherent. An incoherent vibrational waveform would be one that lacks order and functions inefficiently, in a diffuse, chaotic manner. We know that incoherent light waves, like those coming from fluorescent lights, TV screens, or computer screens, can fatigue our system and make us less focused over a period of time.[10] Incoherent vibrational patterns can detrimentally affect how easily we learn and grow, and, in the extreme case, even cause severe damage to our bodies.

The difference between coherent and incoherent light vibrations can be understood by comparing a simple light bulb to a laser. A regular 25 watt light bulb gives off photons of light in a very diffuse, incoherent manner with no set pattern. This incoherent light will light the page we read and give off a little heat but nothing more. However, if we take that same light bulb and get all the photons vibrating at the same frequency in a unified pattern (coherence), we produce a powerful, efficient laser that can cut through steel. The light is now pure, focused, and far more efficient and powerful than when it was incoherent. Similarly, coherence provides us with focus, power and brilliance in our lives.

Interestingly, the ancient Hawaiians believed that all humans were born as bowls of pure light with great power or manna to live their lives harmoniously and creatively. If, during their lives, they interrupted that pure light by putting stones or "pohaku" (incoherent thoughts, words, and actions that disconnected their true nature from that of others and

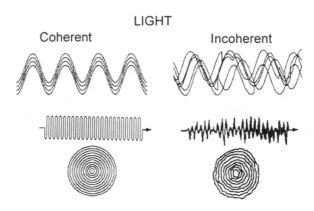

Figure 1.3: Coherent and Incoherent Light

their environment) in their bowls, their light became diffuse, making their lives less harmonious and powerful. The Hawaiians felt that through reconnection and congruity with their light nature, they could simply turn their bowls over causing the stones to drop out and bring their lives back to that coherent pure light. Through understanding coherence, the terms "Enlightenment and Illumination" have taken on the meaning of harmoniously reconnecting to my pure light form, or of my human nature returning to coherence.

Coherent Connection

Especially important to the discussion of this book are the heart and brain waves of the people in our environment. We are in constant communication with one another and continually influence one another through these invisible vibrational fields from our hearts and brains. When these fields are coherent there is a natural sense of safety, belonging and peace, and we feel in harmony with one another. When there is underlying fear due to a perceived or real lack of safety, incoherence inhibits our natural passion, curiosity, and growth.

During play, we exist in a state of total coherence/pleasure, in the most natural learning state available to us. To truly understand coherence, play with a young child—and *let the child lead*. Release time, control, worry, the past and the future. Exist purely in the moment and notice how harmoniously connected you become with your intricate world, seeing with undeterred vision, curiosity and joy.

Children are Zen masters of play, optimally learning and setting in place the perfect mental/emotional structures for a creative life. The blueprint for life-long success is this child-like state where we are totally engrossed in the moment to moment wonder of the world, and our interactions with others, from an ego-less place of total connection. Given a rich, stress-free environment, we are all natural sponges, gently experiencing each new moment, event or object with intense curiosity. Our whole system is finely calibrated to take in and attempt to make sense of each new wonder. In this state we are perfect learners, living in the now—our eyes, ears, touch receptors fully engaged, sensuously scanning each detail, hue, sound, and it may take all afternoon, but time is irrelevant.

Mihalyi Czikszentmihalyi coined the term "FLOW" for this state of coherence. For creativity to occur, he believes there must be an early keen curiosity about one's surroundings, rich experiences and awe about the mysteries of life, plus parental (or adult) support and love—all elements of coherence and pleasure.[11]

The Delicate Child Heart

Childhood took on new meaning as I re-experienced it as a mother to my daughter Breeze. She was conceived in a beautiful Colorado mountain meadow brilliant with August columbine, cinquefoil, rockrose, lupine, and Indian paintbrush. Jim and I, lost in the fresh mountain air, the awesome beauty of the majestic mountainside and each other, had joyously celebrated our union. It was a perfectly coherent way to honor a new soul into existence.

Like so many babies born today and even with her glorious beginning, Breeze was an "accident". Working together in the Biology Department at a local college, Jim and I had fallen deeply in love and had moved in together (as was the custom of the times). Our common passion for biology, learning, and the out-of-doors had woven itself into a wondrous friendship, and our times together were rich. But my unexpected pregnancy severely challenged our relationship.

Jim's first failed marriage was the result of an unexpected pregnancy, so our situation rekindled his fears. The wounds from giving up his two daughters had left deep scars, and he didn't want this baby adding more scars. I, on the other hand, was with a man I loved and trusted deeply, and I wanted this baby. In the mid 60's I had given up a baby for adoption. This was one of the hardest decisions of my life, and I didn't want to go through it again. Though both Jim and I had differing emotions, we loved one another enough to set aside our fears and commit to raising our child as a married couple.

Yet, as our unborn child developed, the fears and uncertainty reemerged, leading to many incoherent days with troubled emotions. Neither of us had any idea that our past individual wounds would be affecting our unborn child who was already developing survival patterns that she would draw on throughout her life.

From the moment she was born, on the eclipse of the full moon, my image of her was that of a red balloon, an explorer of the universe, my guide to worlds forgotten or not yet seen. In her first years, the coherence of two devoted parents and neighbors seemed to buffer the incoherence of my pregnancy and the relationship difficulties Jim and I shared. Jim's path and my path separated when Breeze was five. The twists and turns of those early years overlaid directly one of the most important developmental periods for Breeze. During that time she was gaining a sense of personal connectedness and safety in the world, of growing her emotional/imaginative self and formulating her early patterns for pleasure and learning.

The incoherence that preceded and accompanied our divorce left all three of us with broken hearts. Jim and I, coming from strong scientific backgrounds, did not trust our hearts to heal the connection. We intellectualized our emotions, pushing them into dark corners where they would attack us when we least expected it. Our pain and struggle had produced heart incoherence, decreasing our ability to reconnect to our pleasure and love for each other or co-create viable solutions.

Breeze, as with all babies and young children, was more affected by our state because her soul job was to monitor the coherence/incoherence of her environment for survival. She would mirror the incoherence she felt with bouts of insatiable crying or acting out. At the time, we attributed her reactions to many things, never to our incoherence.

Breeze's wounds weren't obvious until our divorce. Then, overnight, she said she needed glasses. This beautiful girl who always had such clear vision, now exhibited severe myopia. Her myopia seemed a strong metaphor for not wanting to see what was happening in her now insecure world.

I became Breeze's primary caregiver, which suited me fine, because Breeze was literally the light of my life, and I took my role as a single mother very seriously. We spent joyous, pleasurable summers at our Montana cabin where both Breeze and I were able to suspend for a time the incoherence of our lives. I can still see her in her blue tutu, knees looped over the trapeze suspended from a short board between two stately larch trees, talking and singing to herself as one fantasy wove into another. She thrived in her fairyland, playing with her friend Willy, finding fairies among the rotted logs draped thick with moss and ferns, or dallying in the gentle stream dappled by the light of a Montana summer. At these times, Breeze existed in total pleasure/coherence, in the most natural state of existence.

Her child-eyes saw everything new, fascinating, unexpected, and complete. Sticks became all sorts of tools, musical instruments, boats, beasts of burden, parts of houses, and even friends. I became a part of her play world through my fascination with her constant discoveries, and at her summons I shared the incredible wonders she had found, suddenly seeing them new for the first time. I doubled as playmate and storyteller and, on some occasions, as consultant. Oh! What a free spirit she was, engrossed in "no time," wandering toward the cabin only when the light had disappeared and her body needed a hug or some warm soup. She didn't miss TV, store bought toys, or amusement parks, but she desperately missed her father. As I worked through my own confusion and sadness, I assumed Breeze, in her childhood innocence, had healed.

Watching Breeze grow and create herself, as every loving parent does, I hoped that she would be happy, curious, creative, passionate, a joyful learner, flexible, honest, honoring of herself and others, confident, loving, and able to take risks. However, these hopes were not so easily realized. According to her teacher, Breeze was not a "good student". She had problems with reading, spelling, and fitting into the established curriculum. My heart ached as she struggled to gain her center and recognize her value during those frustrating times. This precious being, so brilliant and sensitive, was lost from pleasure and herself. I saw her innate enthusiasm to learn and her bright curious spirit begin to erode, leaving her fearful and uncertain.

I felt I had made many mistakes in "raising" her. I left the confusion in Denver and moved us to Hawaii, changing radically everything that was familiar to her. Changing schools left her feeling she could never catch up, and she lost much of her motivation to succeed. Making new friends suddenly became a scary proposition for this previously confident extrovert. But probably the greatest mistake I made was losing faith in her and myself as I compared her to what a misguided society said was an "A" student.

My over concern for her success, as well as unrealistic academic standards, threatened her belief in herself as an intelligent person and disconnected us from each other. Jim also played his part in this drama. His other two daughters, both good students, graduated from prestigious East Coast schools. Not wanting her to have unrealistic expectations, he lovingly told Breeze that she was probably not college material. This, coming from her father, decreased her connection with him. I clearly saw the effects in her because they reflected my own childhood wounds and disconnection from the pleasure in my life. Most of us have experienced similar or more devastating scenarios in growing up that made it difficult to access the beautiful, unlimited, passionate spirits we authentically are.

Steps Toward Coherence

As I look back over the dynamic interplay of both Breeze's and my life, there are some crucial elements that saved us by assisting our growth toward coherence:

1. an early loving and supportive community (neighborhood);
2. the close connection, love, and trust between each other;
3. a willingness to play, imagine and be childlike together;
4. a strong base of music;
5. the ability to fully communicate with each other;
6. our love of co-creating ideas and physically manifesting them in our lives;
7. the rich sensory environments of Montana and Hawaii; and

8. the remarkable resilience and drive of the human mind/body/ spirit to come to coherence and heal.

Now that neither Breeze nor I care if she gets A's, she gets them easily in her university classes. She continues to expand my world with her profound insights and touch my heart and others with her honest, loving nature. She passionately loves to learn, especially about interactive human nature as an anthropology/sociology major. She finds great pleasure in courses that broaden and deepen her understanding of the human spirit.

As a keen observer, Breeze grows from a conscious understanding of her own life. Her compassion has allowed her to see past the pain and confusion to her potential. In expanding her potential, she uses a formula, one anchored in trusting her own intuition, being conscious and present, being eagerly curious about everyone and everything, and daring to risk and physically taking action to change her mind and reality.

In my work and life, I see our society floundering in its ability to create family, to welcome into belonging each unique individual and support the body, mind, and soul of that individual. Few adults have tools to maintain coherence in their lives and to find their own unique brilliance let alone that of those around them. This fracturing of the human spirit may be our greatest challenge to a bright future.

Coherence applies to our relationships and interactions with family and all the individuals that grace our world. Do we give compassionate, coherent messages and follow through with integrity, impeccably "walking our talk"? Are we able to be coherently present, fully in the moment with another person? Are we able to set clear, humane boundaries with our children and others that support our purpose and theirs?

"Coherence is personal power through increasing one's integrity, understanding and capacity for compassion".[12]

—*David Hawkins*

Being conscious of when we are in a coherent or incoherent state is an important step in being our authentic selves. Researchers in a worldwide study of consciousness have delineated the important links that structure our reality:

"*Consciousness itself is a psychological phenomenon, in that it is the direct experience by the individual of his or her own being. Consciousness enables the individual to reflect upon and interpret experience (including the experience of personal cognition), to construct a sense of self, and to predict and deliberate upon the future. Through these psychological processes, the individual is empowered to pose fundamental ontological and metaphysical questions about reality and individual existence, and potentially construct a sense of meaning and purpose in relation to them. Such construction allows the individual to place a value upon his or her life and the life of others, an activity which is augmented by the ability of consciousness to respond reflectively to the individual's personal world of emotions and feelings, and to conceptualize it in terms of positive or negative effect.*"[13]

Our experiences set the groundwork for how we live our lives, AND we have the choice and dynamic ability, as continually developing individuals, to change our reality. We are all woven from the same fabric with the same need to return to coherence.

To become more coherent — conscious — enlightened is the greatest gift anyone can give to the world; it assures increased pleasure, integrity, creativity, understanding, and compassion.

We all have our wounding and we all long for joy and connection. This is a "How to come back to pleasure and coherence, without drugs, expensive therapy, high tech machines, shopping sprees or even chocolate" book.

In the next chapters, explore with me the stones in our bowls and those of our children that bring about incoherence. They also show us how to remove those stones and reestablish a pure, natural, focused light of coherence in our lives—the child heart.

CHAPTER TWO

Survival or Just Plain Stress?

"But however much the neo-cortex assumes control, the primal brain will still be primal in the sense of being first in importance. It is the primal brain which gives us the urge to survive as an individual..."
—*Michelle Odent*[1]

From a biological perspective, our body's primary function is to protect us, allowing us to survive as long as possible. Our elegant survival apparatus gets set up in utero as the embryo keenly monitors the world around it for danger. Signals from the mother's physical and emotional state set up intricate patterns in the brain that will assure survival. However, they also set an internal gauge of how we will respond to the situations of our life and whether we can easily maintain coherence or not. Our survival patterns keep us alive; make us hyperaware of every potentially dangerous sound, light change, or movement in our environment; and teach us which actions or people are safe.

However, stress is different than survival. It's that insidious state where we indiscriminately pump adrenalin and cortisol through our bodies, where we consciously or subconsciously equate frustrating experiences in our lives with life threatening survival situations. Stress is an aberation of our survival patterning and, if used on a regular basis (chronically), harms every aspect of our life. Both survival and stress set up incoherent patterns in the heart/brain complex, allowing for quick reactions to danger, but decreasing the system's ability to learn, remember or create. Since children take all their cues from us on how to survive and how to live, if the cues come from a parent in chronic stress, the child is surrounded by incoherence, and everything else plays into that.

Stress often becomes the "normal" state for some children, just as it has become the status quo with adults in our society.

STRESS IS:

≈   *useless for actual survival because it depletes and harms the body;*

≈   *the inhibitor of our freedom to risk and grow physically, emotionally, spiritually, and intellectually;*

≈   *the progenitor of depression, hyperactivity, memory loss; learning difficulties, and horrible diseases like AIDS, cancer, and multiple sclerosis;*

≈   *the activator of alienating behaviors which isolate us from love, belonging, and altruism;*

≈   *the detractor of our natural drive to explore, learn, and add to the beauty and wonder of our world through pleasure and our creative endeavors.*

Why on earth would we make stress such a center-post of our lives? I honestly ask myself this question a lot. How did we get off track, misusing our elegant survival mechanism for everything in our daily lives?

If I'm going to really be present and free in every moment to be authentically myself, I have to step out of the grip of stress and open up to every moment with full vulnerability and wonder, with all the innocence of the child mind.

I think I was a fairly innocent kid, oblivious to the stresses of the world, joyful with my life and everyone in it, until my hormones started to change at the same time mom's did (she was 40 when I was born). There seemed to be a sort of domino effect. As mom's stress levels elevated (she was also renewing her teaching certificate at the university and substitute teaching at the time), dad's impatience increased, which he turned on me by finding fault with everything I did. I felt disconnection from both mom and dad, and in my over-sensitized hormonal state, I became a belligerent teenager with my stress cycle full blown. From that time until recently, my underlying stress has centered on the disconnection, especially with my father.

As I now look at my fall from innocence into stress, it's laughable and tragic at the same time. I held a lot of anger toward my dad for many years, missing this man who was a noted journalist, writer of poetry, photographer, avidly curious traveler, lover of beauty, and caretaker and lover of me. If, at the time we had known ways to come back to coherence with each other and ourselves, our time together would have become precious encounters valued for a lifetime. The stress in our relationship, instead, disconnected us from our love for each other.

I am now becoming more aware of when I am stressed—recognizable through the locked knees, tight shoulders, eyes that won't focus right, and jumbled speech patterns. Having taught about the effects of chronic stress on the body to worldwide audiences, I am hit with the old axiom, "We teach what we most need to learn." I am keenly aware of the dangers to my life of hectic schedules, constant air travel, jet lag, and unreasonable deadlines set up to still prove to dad, who died in 1988, that I am valuable and worthy of his love. When I am not oblivious, I can actually see the origin of the pattern and use the tools I have learned to stop the stress reaction. But when I was pregnant with Breeze, and in those first five developmental years following her birth, I had no such awareness.

Setting the Stage — Hurry Up!

"Today's child has become the unwilling, unintended victim of overwhelming stress. The stress borne of rapid, bewildering social change and constantly rising expectations."[2]
—David Elkin

Because babies and children are so adept at taking their cues from us, it may be time to examine our patterns of behavior. In my workshops and presentations I ask if people experience stress in their lives, and they all answer, "YES". Then I ask about daily, ongoing stress in the form of worry, fear, or frustration, and they also answer, "YES", as if that were natural. Chronic stress is not natural, but it has become the norm and sets the stage for the emotional, physical, and social ailments in our lives, those of our children and of the world in general.

We are missing "down time" and intimate close time with others in our hurried society. Consider all the activities you and/or your family participate in during a typical week. What percentage of the time is spent in relatively high intensity activities like getting to work, school, and extracurricular activities; shopping; competitive sports; or confrontations? What is the percentage spent in physically inactive, high intensity activities like watching TV, cruising the Internet, or playing a video game? What percentage is spent on active, low intensity, personal connection activities like taking a walk; swimming or bike riding alone or with a friend, partner or child; imaginative/spontaneous play; reading a book, gardening, doing yoga or Tai Chi; meditating? What about the percentage of activities that should be low intensity and personally connecting but are not because they are hurried (interacting with your family: making or eating meals; doing housework, yard-work, or homework; putting a child to bed).[3] In many families, high intensity and hurried are the norm.

In our "hurried" society, everything seems to be evaluated by either efficiency or economy—"how much work did I get done today or how much money did I make?" This greatly affects how we see ourselves. I wonder if our whole society is attempting, at some level, to prove their worth and lovability to their fathers, mothers, etc. My stress was always focused around expectations I had for myself and the ones I thought others had for me, thus pushing me to meet performance standards or other people's wishes. For me, it meant becoming a professional mom, having skills or demands in both areas, and attempting to do it all to perfection. The stresses Breeze and her generation are dealing with are similar but seem to be far more difficult. Her generation may be dealing with the fallout of our habitual hurriedness.

Today, creativity, craftsmanship, tenacity, and wisdom are being replaced by the fast and the cheap, so things wear out quickly and are thrown away rather than fixed. This has broad implications for our environment as a throw away, environmentally polluting society. It can also spill over into our personal relationships with throwaway relationships, high divorce rates and split families. We move from one thing to the next, from one relationship to the next, seeking new and more intense stimuli while missing the quality and connection.

The Passive Stress of TV and Computers

Our natural survival response makes us acutely aware of danger signals in our environment. Television is one such stimulator of stress through its danger signals. Whenever there is a sudden light change in our environment, the brain immediately perceives it as danger, like the light change that would occur if a wild animal came out of the forest at us. TV programmers are hired to keep people watching, so they build in lots of light changes which signal danger in the brain and keep people watching. You can see these light changes when you walk by a home at night that has the TV turned on.[4] You also see light changes on a video of a computer screen.

If the danger signal is constantly there, and there is no way to fight or flee, we go into "freeze" mode and attempt to block it out. Watch a person watching TV. The zombie like staring is the only defense available. Just the "brain strain" of forming 625 lines composed of over 800 dots appearing twenty-five times per second into meaningful images is considerable, let alone the light changes. Watching TV we receive direct danger signals to the body, flooding the system with stress chemicals. We can't fight the TV, and we can't leave, so we block out the stimuli by staring.

TV advertising, geared to increase consumerism, knows of our blockout attempts, so they increase the sensory intensity to regain our attention by making the commercials louder with more light changes. Staring, with its lack of eye movement, can produce sleeplessness, anxiety, nightmares, headaches, perceptual disorders, poor concentration, and blunted senses.[5] Over time, the body gets accustomed to the stimuli and expects increased stimulation, and we become a nation with "stimuli addiction".[6]

We have become a culture constantly saturated with overwhelming stimuli from the bright lights and loud sounds in eating establishments, large superstores, malls, mass transportation, movie theaters, amusement parks, and even grocery stores. With each excursion to high stimuli areas, we set up an unconscious need for even more heightened sensory stimulation;[7] we become addicted. Our heightened sensory need causes us to dose ourselves with caffeinated drinks, media fixes, sports events, extreme sports, and/ or constantly filled agendas.[8]

Our hyperactivity (reactivity), the inability to be peaceful and fully present, focused, and connected with others or a situation) exemplifies our state of chronic stress.[9,10] Many people even believe there is good stress (eustress) and bad stress (distress), which may merely be a way of justifying our "stress addiction". Our physiology only has two settings: either we are in survival (stressed), or we are not.

During stress we miss the first hand, rich sensory experience of nature and each other. Very telling are the figures that heart disease and depression are our top two diseases, that 65 million Americans are diagnosed with mild to severe anxiety disorders and consume more than 5 billion doses of tranquilizers and sleeping pills per year.[11]

Because we seldom take quiet, reflective downtime, our children don't value "down time", feeling bored if there is a lull in the stimulation. We all miss the joy of interactive activities like unstructured play, explorations in nature, singing, dancing, drawing, creating and reading or being read to. We become entrained to chronic stress patterns, and our hyperactive, stimulus bound existence is simply a reflection of our hurried, stressed out society.[12]

It is time to ask what is most dear to us. To find an answer that includes pleasure and coherent connection with other people, a wonder and curiosity about the mysteries of life, and a commitment to joy and learning requires being aware of and managing our stress.

A Self-Administered Stress Test

The very best way to understand the concept of stress is to have a personal body awareness of what is happening. Experiencing what is happening in your body during stress provides a concrete reference point for much of the information in this book. From this exercise, you may find, as I did, that you are in chronic stress more often than you realize.

Think of a frustrating situation in your life and become totally aware of the changes in your whole body.

Check off the things you notice:

___   fast shallow breathing or you stopped breathing

___   faster heart beat

___   unsettled stomach, cramps, feeling nauseous

___   locked knees

___   Tightened muscles: ___ neck ___ jaw ___ arms ___ legs ___ lower back ___ forehead

Where is the weight on your feet? ___ balls ___ heels ___ sides ___ uneven
(explain _____)

Lean over and touch your toes/floor/ or whatever and notice how far you can go. ___ Any tightness in lower back with this activity?

Turn your head to the right and left as far as you can without moving the rest of your body. Notice your range of motion by noticing how far you can see.

Tightness in neck: ___ right side ___ left side

Check your eyes to see if there is any muscle tightness when you look: ___ up ___ down ___ right ___ left ___ cross your eyes

Track the eyes back and forth: _____ difference of range of motion on one side _____ jumpy

Read a paragraph from the book once and notice your level of comprehension _____% _____ eyes jumpy or tired.

Stop—don't take that pill!! Here are a few physical activities that will work 100 times better in the long run and give you simple ways to stop the stress reaction.

A FEW STRESS RELEASE ACTIVITIES:

≈   Focus on what is RIGHT with your life; write out a gratitude list of things you are thankful for.

≈   Take a 15-minute or longer walk in nature, focusing on your surroundings, the colors, sounds, smells, and feel of the air.

≈   Put on a favorite audiotape or CD and dance to it.

≈   Do some Tai Chi or Yoga

≈ Touch your right elbow to your left knee and then the left elbow to the right knee in a slow, conscious, relaxed manner—(cross crawl from Brain Gym®)

Figure 2.1: HookUps from Brain Gym ®

≈ Stand, sit, or lie in Hook Up's from Brain Gym®. (Cross one ankle over the other, then extend your arms with thumbs down, cross your wrists and entwine your fingers. Then roll your entwined hands under to rest on your chest. Rest your tongue on the roof of your mouth. Relax your shoulders away from your ears and focus on your breathing and heart rhythm).[13]

≈ Sing your favorite song, either acapella or with an audiotape or CD.

Now go back and recheck if there is any difference in your breathing, heart rate, stomach, muscle tension, back of the knees, weight on the feet, eye movements and comprehension. Check your range of motion by leaning over to touch the floor and move your head from side to side.

These activities help integrate the whole mind/body system and reduce the stress reaction. You may have noticed that if you have a problem, taking a walk (even down the hall of your office building) will change your perspective and allow you to come up with some feasible solutions. Do you notice a change in the way you now view the frustrating situation? Usually the frustration does not appear as threatening, and often, greater understanding and even solutions become available.

Movement, especially if it's cross lateral (touching one hand to the opposite leg across the midline of the body) and done slowly and consciously, mechanically activates the whole brain, thus overriding the limited brain function of the survival reaction. Research is showing that the best way to change our minds and physiology is through taking ACTION. The following sign I saw on a bus says it all!

"STRESS WON'T STICK TO A MOVING TARGET."

Why Be Coherent — the Physiology of Stress

We hear a lot about the importance of reducing our stress. But sometimes it helps to really understand why stress is so physically, mentally, and emotionally damaging to us. Having a Western scientific orientation, I tend to want the reasons behind why I am doing something. The following helped me get a handle on why my life depends on my changing my stress habit NOW.

Physiologically, what people experience from doing the stress test explains so much of our instant reactions to the situations in our lives. In a short-term survival situation, our bodies work optimally for sharper focus, memory, and strength. However, when we maintain a survival state for a longer period of time (more than the time it would take to save ourselves from a real life threatening situation), survival becomes stress. Survival is our ally, but stress threatens our health, damages our bodies, and inhibits our ability to learn and grow.[14]

When we experience fear, frustration, anger, or any threat, parts of the brain begin a complex process that produces the stress response all over our bodies. The hypothalamus (a brain structure that lies right above the pituitary gland) sends a nerve impulse to the sympathetic nervous system. The sympathetic nervous system, a part of our autonomic (automatic rather than conscious) nervous system, stimulates the adrenal glands to secrete adrenalin. At the same time, the hypothalamus steps up production of corticotropin-releasing factor (CRF). CRF induces the pituitary gland to secrete ACTH (adreno-corticotrophic hormone), which in turn instructs the adrenal glands to secrete cortisol. The adrenal glands, the source organ for adrenalin and cortisol, lie above the kidneys.[15]

ADRENALIN is an information chemical in the body that causes your heart rate to increase, makes breathing shallow and quick, and diverts blood to the big muscles of the arms and legs so you can fight or flee. In the fight or flight state, the back of the knees lock to protects your Achilles tendon from being torn (tendon guard reflex).[16] However, if we don't take the action of fighting or fleeing, the locked knees unbalance the body, causing the back and neck muscles to tighten in order to hold us up right. (You may have noticed the weight on the balls of your feet as you over-focus on the stress, attempting to figure it out or fight it. Or you may have noticed the weight on the heels of your feet, as you felt overwhelmed and ready to run).

In our attempt to keep control and appear "cool", the muscles of the lower back have to constantly maintain our balance, pulling on the vertebrae, which over time causes back problems, even herniated discs. Stress is so chronic in the U.S. that 80% of the population eventually experiences lower back (lumbar) pain, with 30 million people hobbled with it at any one time. Even in people who have no signs of lower back problems, disk abnormalities including herniations, show up on MRI scans in 64% of people tested. Another sign of chronic stress![17]

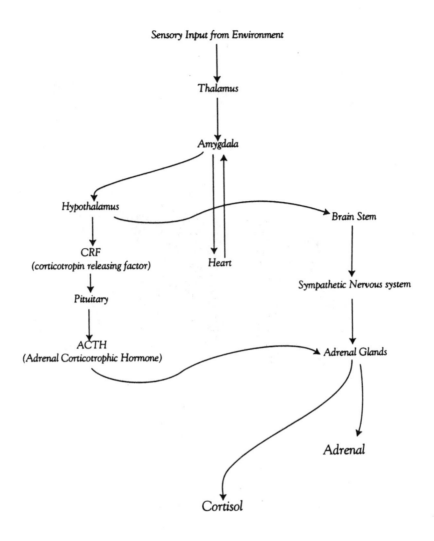

Figure 2.2: Hormonal Stress Reaction

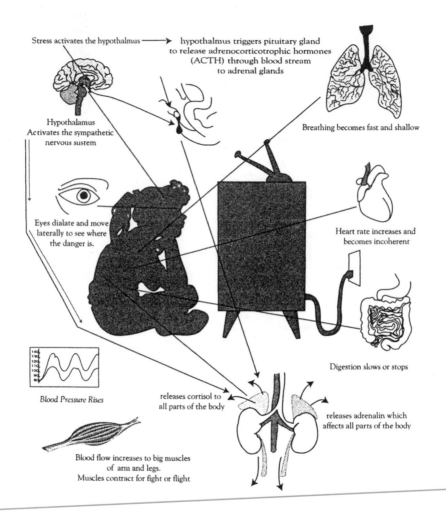

Stress activates the hypothalmus ──▶ hypothalmus triggers pituitary gland
to release adrenocorticotrophic hormones
(ACTH) through blood stream
to adrenal glands

Hypothalamus
Activates the sympathetic
nervous sustem

Breathing becomes fast and shallow

Eyes dialate and move
laterally to see where
the danger is.

Heart rate increases and
becomes incoherent

Digestion slows or stops

Blood Pressure Rises

releases cortisol to
all parts of the body

releases adrenalin which
affects all parts of the body

Blood flow increases to big muscles
of arm and legs.
Muscles contract for fight or flight

Figure 2.3: Physiological Reaction to Stress

The tendon guard reflex also inhibits our normal flexibility to walk, sit, dance, run, play sports, and lean over to touch our toes. (You probably noticed more relaxed knees and were able to bend over further after doing the stress release activities.)

As the lower back tightens during stress, so do the neck and shoulder muscles, getting you ready to fight. With chronic stress, the contracted muscles push on the underlying veins, like the jugular vein, and inhibit normal blood flow out of the head. This can result in inflammation of the brain or meninges resulting in migraine headaches. Tight neck muscles vastly reduce the range of motion, giving us chronic stiff necks and tension headaches.[18]

The temporal mandibular joint (TMJ where the lower jaw comes into the upper jaw just in front of the ear) tightens to protect your jaw from injury during an attack.

There are more nerves coming across the TMJ than any other joint in the body. These cranial nerves affect all the sensory input from the face to the brain, plus movement of the eyes, mouth, tongue and other facial parts. Tightening of the TMJ limits facial expression, seeing, chewing, and vocalization. Some people have problems from grinding their teeth or not being able to open their mouths wide. Yawning and massaging the temporal mandibular joint at the same time is great for helping to release the tight muscles.[19]

The muscles of the eyes are also affected by adrenalin. The eyes dilate to take in maximal light and focus laterally (turning outward) to enable you to see where the threat lies in your periphery.[20] With chronic stress the outer eye muscles tend to become stronger over time, and the inner eye muscles become weak. With weak inner eye muscles, it will be hard to converge or cross your eyes. In order to read effectively, both eyes must be able to converge on a page of writing and work together in synchrony. When you attempt to read while stressed, your dominant eye will be checking the periphery for danger and your non-dominant eye will do the reading since reading is secondary to survival. Because the eyes aren't working together they may tire easily, and comprehension may decrease so you have to read a sentence over and over before it makes any sense.

Adrenalin also inhibits energy intensive food digestion, so energy can be directed to running from our modern-day saber-toothed tigers. Gastric distress, acid indigestion, stomach problems, or ulcers are indicators of chronic stress, and the market is flooded with advertising and pharmaceutical helps for these prevalent complaints.

The Brain and Stress

The term "half cocked" applies to the stressed brain. The parts of the brain that have to do with reaction and moving the muscles in flight or fight take over. Blood flow decreases to the higher areas of the brain that have to do with planning, creativity and insight. Brain function becomes homolateral (one sided) as the non-dominant hemisphere receives less blood flow. This may allow the dominant hemisphere to more efficiently direct the survival reaction without having to consult across the corpus callosum with the other hemisphere. The brain goes into a fast Beta brain wave pattern that facilitates reaction and movement, while alpha and theta waves for thinking and learning decrease. *(note figure 2.4)*

The left Pre-Frontal Cortex, an area of the brain just behind the forehead, which is responsible for maintaining positive feelings and inhibiting negative emotions, also shuts down, allowing the threat to drive the body through the stress reaction.[21]

Our dominant hemisphere determines how we will react in order to survive. If our lead function is the Gestalt (usually right) hemisphere, we will likely respond emotionally to the overall situation rather than the details. The right prefrontal cortex, working intimately with the amygdala, increases the levels of negative, threat filled emotions.[22] It becomes hard to see the world as a safe place, and because the logic hemisphere is mostly shut down, we have a hard time explaining in a logical, verbal way what is going on with us. In the book, *The Indigo Children*, it is suggested that people with learning difficulties (ADD, ADHD, Emotionally Handicapped) are more likely to be gestalt dominant.[23] This holds with my earlier findings, elaborated in my book, *The Dominance Factor*.[24]

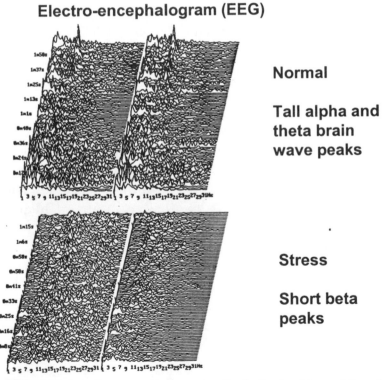

NORMAL INTEGRATED BRAIN FUNCTION   STRESS REACTION

frontal lobes

back brain

Positron Emmission Tomography(PET) showing major areas of activity across the brain.[25]

Electro-encephalogram (EEG)

Normal

Tall alpha and theta brain wave peaks

Stress

Short beta peaks

Figure 2.4: PET and EEG Scans of the Brain During Normal Function and Stress. This PET scan and EEG show how the blood flow to the whole brain decreases, going only to the areas having to do with survival.[1]

If our lead function is the logic (usually left) hemisphere, we will tend to focus on the details, unable to see the forest for the trees. Because the left pre-frontal cortex modulates the amygdala's negative emotions, its reaction may be more one of figuring out specifically what is going on, rather than getting emotionally involved. Since the verbal linguistic center lies in the logic hemisphere, the inclination may be to talk in an attempt to understand all the parts of the situation, resulting in action that is too late. Or missing the big picture, the logic hemisphere often comes up with band-aid solutions which lack understanding or the real or deeper meaning and therefore don't really work.

The survival response in a dangerous situation is usually a very quick, short-term reaction, so working with limited brain function does not usually pose a problem. But when we live in chronic (fairly constant and/or long-term) stress, we put ourselves at a great disadvantage. Being stressed out is like attempting to keep a ball in the air with one eye shut, one hand behind our back, and hopping on one foot. Learning, planning, creativity and just life itself become more difficult and limited.

Cortisol — A Double-Edged Sword

Cortisol, the other stress hormone, is released from the cortex of the adrenal glands to stimulate the breakdown of body tissues, which provide energy for fight or flight. Because of its devastating effect on the body, cortisol is the stress hormone that most frightens me. Under chronic stress, the effects of cortisol include the following:

≈   It blocks efficient metabolism of glucose and breaks down tissue, including bone, increasing the danger of osteoporosis.[26, 27] Stressed pre-menopausal women develop bones as porous as those of post-menopausal women.[28]

≈   It inhibits the uptake of proteins by as much as 70%, leaving decreased protein for building strong muscles and nerve networks.

≈   It causes the release of fat into the blood, which under chronic conditions isn't used for the action of fight or flight but accumulates, especially around the waist and hips, resulting in obesity.[29] Currently, half of all Americans are classified as overweight.[30]

≈   It causes nerve cells, especially of the hippocampus (the brain area that helps to formulate memory after receiving input from other brain regions), to lose their dendritic branches and spines and eventually die off, resulting in poor memory, fuzzy thinking, and lack of creativity.[31, 32, 33]

≈   It depresses the immune system, lowering imunoglobulin levels, and has been deemed the most violent immunodepressant known to man. Chronic stress elevates cortisol levels while decreasing the levels of dehydroepiandrosterone (DHEA) which plays a key role in our immune system. This decrease in DHEA occurs because cortisol and DHEA have the same building blocks (progesterone and pregnenolone). Stress causes these building blocks to be channeled into making cortisol, thus decreasing DHEA and disabling our body's immune system.[34] High cortisol and low DHEA levels are found in people with major diseases such as AIDS, MS, diabetes, cancer, coronary artery disease, and Alzheimer's disease.[35]

≈   It causes the blood cells responsible for clotting (platelets) to become stickier to protect from blood loss in the case of wounding. Heart attack occurs because increased blood pressure causes a crack to develop in the artery lining that covers a fatty plaque. Then platelets, drawn to the site, instantly adhere in their stickier state to the artery wall and aggregate, choking off blood flow to the heart.[36]

≈   It is especially high in children with parental loss, long-standing emotional separation from parents or insecure relationships with their parents. This causes a weakening of young children's biological stress-response system.[37] A study of stressed macaque monkey mothers correlates with what we are seeing in humans. The Macaque mothers became emotionally distant from their infants. The young monkeys, in turn exhibited elevated levels of cortisol, expressed fear in new settings, became distressed if separated briefly from their mothers, and were socially inept with their peers.[38]

≈   It leads to *depression*, fatigue, muscle pain, high blood pressure, ulcers, short stature, and fertility problems.[39]

≈   It is described as a form of slow physiological suicide. A high cortisol/low DHEA ratio leads to premature aging.[40]

We often unknowingly stimulate cortisol production through our media, worry, foods, and caffeinated beverages. We also encourage people to talk about their problems over and over again. However, one study shows that just *5 minutes* of talking about or expressing the anger around a stressor, raises cortisol levels in the blood for *6 hours*.[41] A good friend, facilitator, counselor or therapist, coherently coming from their heart, empowers us to move past the anger and come up with workable solutions rather than remaining in the stress state.

As adults, we can't provide the peace and security required in order to develop the child heart in children if we are in frequent stress, for children pick up our stress like sponges. Stress also overrides the growth of our own child heart and thus our ultimate joy in life. One of the most insidious outcomes of stress is depression, with its isolation being a destroyer of the child heart.

CHAPTER THREE

Depression—Sign of Our Times

"Loneliness and depression are the diseases of the West."
—*Mother Theresa*

Depression is yet another side affect of our hurried, stressed out, unconnected society. Approximately 3.4 million young people under age 18 and 10 million adults in the U.S. experience "serious" depression each year. The American Psychiatry Association claims that 1 out of 4 women, and 1 out of 10 men experience depression which, at its current rate is projected to be the number one disease in the U.S. and number two in the world by the year 2020.[1]

Tribal Africans have a solid family/clan structure that assures everyone is taken care of and belongs. These people live by "Ubuntu" which means, *"Because I am, we are, and because we are, I am."* We are more ruggedly individualistic in our Western culture, which can easily lead to a sense of isolation, loneliness, and depression. Thus we are at least three to five times more likely to get sick and die prematurely, not only from heart disease, but from all causes. Dean Ornish claims that nothing more powerfully affects our health than love, connection and community.[2]

Depression is most frequent when people constantly rethink the event without an effective way to emotionally experience and express it.[3] In traditional Chinese teachings, emotions are considered the driving energy of the body, necessary for life, while the spirit and social training control their manifestations.[4] In our society that touts "cool headed" intellectualism, there is no *real* emotional action we can take to stress, or joy for that matter,[5] so we tend to "armor" ourselves. It is a way to suppress our feelings or actions by tightening the muscles that would normally express them. It shows up in tight jaws (inhibiting verbal expression), shoulder problems (inhibiting the fight reaction), and low back problems (inhibiting the flee reaction). People learn early to construct their "armor" if their emotions have no outlet. The chronic tension of "armoring" limits mobility and the ability to feel, thus, we begin to get out of touch with our bodies, and our inner and physical natures. Rigid muscles impede the flow of energy throughout the body, so the system becomes depressed.[6] Depression becomes the body's way of withdrawing to conserve energy and minimize risk.

During depression the left PFC (pre-frontal cortex), with its ability to focus on the positive, decreases its function as does the amygdala. In depressed people, the ventral anterior cingulate that connects the left PFC to the hypothalamus and orchestrates the hormonal response that assures fight or flee, is 40% smaller, so depressed people do nothing.[7, 8]

Within weeks of depressive stress, the hippocampus wears out as the spines on its neurons wither and the cells die, hindering its ability to tell the hypothalamus to stop delivering more stress hormones, thus stress rises.[9] The communication breakdown between the prefrontal cortex and the amygdala distorts emotional responses and the social decisions one makes.[10] In violent men and schizophrenics the hippocampus and amygdala are smaller by as much as 19%.[11]

Depressed people tend to have few social contacts and become negative about the people around them, making relationships difficult. They don't feel like they fit in and have little curiosity about other people or new ideas, so they become antisocial and isolated. The isolation leads to low self-esteem, a lost sense of value, and even self-abuse.[12] People are only mean when they've forgotten their own value.

Isolation has become a way of life for many children and adults in our society. TV and computers become focal areas for the families, decreasing first hand interactive communication or real play and touch. Parents are busy earning a living, often leaving latchkey kids, who are missing family warmth and connection and we experience the consequences in the form of violence. As adults, isolation and our longing for self value and connection often take the form of obsessive consumerism, necessitating that we work more and leave our families more. Thus the cycle of isolation continues.

Real Life Depression

I hadn't really thought much about depression until I met Catherine Carrigan. She had survived years of depression, with its ensuing suicide attempts, going from one drug therapy to another and from one therapist to the next. She ended up in one of my courses because she had discovered that she could stop the depression through the integrated movements of Brain Gym® and wanted to know more. It sparked my interest, and I began reading the studies, studies that tied right back into our culture's "stress addiction."[13]

Then Breeze went through a bout of depression, and I got a first hand experience of how debilitating it can be. Breeze, who is highly sensitive and emotional, was hit with a semester filled with incoherence. She had enrolled in Deviant Behavior, a course where she studied Marilyn Manson in depth; Black Literature, a course elucidating the immense struggles of African Americans; and Abnormal Psychology. On top of this, she was acting a very strong but dark role in a play as Circe, in a modernized version of Homer's Odyssey. She would come home from school to her roommate's exploration (as an art major) of dark art which hung all over their apartment. Breeze was also working part time which sapped her energy and left her little time for intimate sharing and contact with friends.

All these influences had taken their toll, and this normally vibrant, joyful being had become overwhelmed and obsessed by her life. She had stepped onto the set of a play, which she felt helpless to change and was making it her reality. She began to isolate herself, she slept instead of going out with friends or exercising in her free time. Her schoolwork and every aspect of her life were suffering.

I was so concerned that I stayed in town and, with my best cajoling, got her to take walks with me. As we walked, we would talk deeply about what was happening in her life and the things she appreciated. The walking gave her an integrated action, which engaged her whole brain, and the talking allowed the emotions to be expressed. Our playfulness with each other helped to bring some humor into her life. We would cuddle as I cleaned her ears —the thing she loves to have me do the most. We went skiing together in the Utah snow and high mountain sunlight, leaving her perception of life, for the glorious present. She began pulling herself together, doing what she knew would change her energy and outlook. Her tenacity and wisdom, love for nature and movement, along with our strong love and connection, brought about her return to the glorious possibilities of her life.

The Depressed Angry Heart

If depressive stress is not managed, violence may be the result. In March of 1999, America was stunned by the incident at Columbine High School in Colorado, as two boys, good students, each from high socio-economic, two-parent families, killed 13 and wounded many other students, then killed themselves. In a special report on "Troubled Kids" in *Time Magazine*, May 31, 1999 the word *depression* kept coming up. Of the nine boys they spotlighted in the article, who had killed other kids and adults, five were considered depressed and three were on Ritalin, Prozac or Luvox.

All of these boys were known to spend long hours on the Internet, playing video games, and listening to dark music. Their favorite video games were Doom, Mortal Kombat, Quake and their music came from Marilyn Manson, Nirvana, and Tupac Shakur. The incoherent content of the video games and music surely had an effect on these young men, desperately attempting to connect with something meaningful that expressed what they were feeling.

Breeze pointed out to me that the anger expressed in the music mirrored the hopeless, helpless sadness they could relate to but were unable to express themselves. They weren't alone in their pain. The Internet also provided them some connection, where they could interact with other people, create a virtual persona, and somehow be part of a community. But the interactions were secondhand, with no touch or movement to ground the connection. Gangs symbolize a form of reaching out for connection in community. Without a community, or other people to relate to, we don't have a sense of being real.

The Isolated Heart

We know that the more social contacts people have, the happier and healthier they are.[14] Our strong ties are those relationships associated with frequent contact, deep feelings of affection and obligation, and a broad base of understanding. Strong ties tend to buffer people from life's stresses and lead to better social and psychological safety.[15]

Television, video games and the Internet markedly decrease social interaction that develop strong ties and establishes a second hand world of experience that makes it difficult to truly connect.[16,17,18,19]. The Columbine killers were very adept at computer games and the Internet. By 1998, approximately 40% of all U.S. households owned a personal computer with one third having Internet access. Carnegie Mellon University set up a study, funded by 13 major computer companies, to examine the effects of the Internet on the social involvement and psychological well being of 169 people in 73 households in Pittsburgh, Pennsylvania, during their first 1 to 2 years on-line.[20]

Though the study group mainly used their computers for communication, the results were telling. Greater use of the Internet was associated with statistically significant declines in social involvement (first-hand or personal communication with family and friends), decrease in the size of a person's local social network, and an increase in loneliness and depression. Internet use affected teenagers more than adults, with greater declines in social support and more loneliness.

Our technology leaves us overwhelmed by volumes of EMAIL, Voice Mail messages, and Faxes, while dramatically infringing on our peace and quality of life.[21] We spend large chunks of time daily, answering EMAIL while missing the first hand experience of being with the flesh, and blood people just a few steps away. And then we wonder why we are lonely!

The poignancy of these young, disenfranchised killers has special meaning for me. When Breeze was 8 months old, I found myself on the other end of that gun, with two boys (maybe 16 years old) telling me they would kill me. They had come into our home, for what, I'm not sure. As they pulled the trigger, they did not see this new mother full of dreams; they only saw the stark fear and, with it, an elegant survival response that moved my body back and barely out of the path of the oncoming bullet. In my panic, I grabbed Breeze, ran and huddled in the bedroom, whispering desperately to the 911 operator, as these two young men coolly jive talked their way out of our back yard. They were totally unaware of the safety they had ripped from my soul, unaware of the spark they had set in my heart to somehow understand their senseless actions, my underlying need to someday piece together the puzzle to somehow protect myself and them.

In our driven society, these young men had exchanged real actions, which elicit a sense of belonging, for an electronic substitute; the intimacy and touch of a friend for the world of Marilyn Manson. The stress of isolation is a killer. We must invite people into life, or they will choose death without connection—to others and themselves. We have no time to leave our future, our precious children, out of our lives and in the hands of an incoherent sensory world.

> *"The human heart can go the length of God – dark and*
> *cold we may be, but this is no winter now.*
> *The frozen misery of centuries breaks, cracks, begins*
> *to move. The thunder is the thunder of the flows, the*
> *thaw, the flood, the upstart Spring.*
> *Thank God our time is now, when wrong comes up to meet us*
> *everywhere—never to leave us till we take the*
> *longest stride of soul men ever took.*
> *Affairs are now soul sized.*
> *THE ENTERPRISE IS EXPLORATION INTO GOD!*
> *But where are you making for? It takes so many*
> *Thousand years to wake. But will you wake – for*
> *pity sake."*
> —*A Sleep of Prisoners*, Christopher Fry[22]

Parenting From The Child Heart

What can we as parents do? Take the time to truly be present with our children, without judgments about their music or outlets to community. Get involved personally, go with our children to concerts, play the video games with them, and then ask, honestly out of curiosity, what is important for them in the music or video game? Listen, listen, listen to this precious being our love created, and then model coherence for them. Honor and mirror back to them their emotions, "I hear that you are feeling very isolated and angry" with empathy. Ask them about their choices and how those choices assist their lives, helping them to feel less stressed, angry or isolated. Listen without judgment and again mirror back their choices "you have chosen to _____ which assists you with _____."

Accept them as exploring, wise individuals, seeking what they need most—a solid sense of themselves. Make them partners in your life, working and playing along side you. Give them options to be of value such as working with younger children, the elderly or animals. Keep offering them healthy outlets as they develop greater responsibility, things that demand constructive action, and a sense of accomplishment. Adolescence is an especially sensitive time when the need for intimacy and to be value through constructive action is paramount. As we trust our kids to learn how to handle themselves, we give them back their power.[23,24]

In all cases, the young men/killers mentioned were physically inactive, so, take the time to move, play, and talk in nature with your child and young adult on a daily basis. Seriously limit or discard TV and computers all together for your children and yourself so they and you have time to share, be creative and have reflective time alone. Do simple, connection-oriented things together, invite their friends to join you, and then celebrate your connection with lots of listening and touch.

Addressing the underlying causes of depression honestly (disconnection from self and others), stopping runaway thought patterns, and getting the body moving and focused on the present can break the depression cycle. If depressive stress is managed, especially with true intimacy, touch, and movement, the spines on the neurons of the hippocampus regrow, and new replacement cells develop.[25,26] When we take the longest stride of soul to be present and listen, our heart coherency will open the way for a deeper understanding on all levels.

CHAPTER FOUR

The Masterful Heart

"And what is as important as knowledge?" asked the mind. "Caring and seeing with the heart", answered the soul.

—Flavia[1]

The heart and mind are seen as one and the same in Traditional Chinese Medicine. The heart is the center of the soul in yogic practice and has long symbolized love and emotions. Western science, until recently, has seen it simply as a complex, tenacious pump and the dreaded target of heart disease. Scientific researchers are now saying, "The heart is a highly complex, self-organized sensory organ with its own functional 'little brain' that communicates with and influences the brain via the nervous system, hormonal system and other pathways."[2]

After all the emphasis on the brain this past decade, the new research on the heart is very exciting. Besides the influence of the heart on brain function, the findings are showing that the quality of our connection to others, especially our family, is a strong indicator of the health of our heart. A forty-two year longitudinal study done with Harvard students demanded that we rethink the heart's function regarding love.

In the study, Harvard students, then in their 20's, were asked a battery of questions. When these same people were interviewed in their mid 60's, an interesting correlation was found between a question asked of them in their 20's and the percentage that had heart disease (Americans number one killer) in later life. The question was: "Do you have one loving parent, two loving parents or no loving parents"? These were the results:

	Percent with Heart Disease
Two Loving Parents	25%
One Loving Parent	35%
No Loving Parents	93%

Also, 100% of the "no loving parents" group had life threatening diseases compared to less than half of the other two groups.[3]

Millions of dollars have gone into studying the "risk factors" of heart disease: high cholesterol diets, high blood pressure, cigarette smoking, obesity, lack of regular exercise, diabetes mellitus and genetic predisposition. However, about half the people who suffer their first heart attack have none of these common risk factors for heart disease. Moreover, more than 8 out of 10 people with at least three of these risk factors never have a heart attack.[4] With the stress of isolation and disconnection from family being a stronger causation of heart disease, it's time to take another look at the heart.

Interestingly, the beat of the heart resides in each of its cells and is controlled within the heart by a pacemaker. Individual heart cells in a petre dish will beat at their own rhythm until they come into close proximity with another cell. They then begin to beat in unison or synchrony with each other, without any kind of innervations from the brain.[5] During a heart transplant, the new heart's pacemaker (SA or sinoatrial node) will spontaneously start the beat of the heart without external help.[6] The function of the brain is simply to regulate the speed of the heartbeat, speeding it up during stress to supply blood to the muscles for fight or flight, or slowing it down during rest.[7] This ability to operate by itself hints that the heart is like a constellation unto itself within the body.

According to Andrew Armour in his book *Neurocardiology*, nerves going from the heart to the brain carry information regarding hormones, chemicals, rate, pressure, pain, and feelings which have a regulatory role over many nerve signals going from the brain back to the heart and other organs. The heart actually appears to have its own sensitivity to the world and exhibits that with intelligence, to the extent that the brain energetically revolves around the heart, not the other way around.[8] Armour's profound statement about the heart led me to delve deeper and change my view of the heart as a simple pump.

One of the most amazing traits of the heart is that it generates an electrical field with an amplitude 60 times greater than the electrical field produced by the brain. The EMF (electro-magnetic field) of the heart, measured externally by a SQUID (superconducting quantum interference device) is at least 1,000 times greater than the field produced by the brain. It is the largest electro-magnetic field in the body extending to a currently measurable distance of 8 - 16 feet (more than 5 meters) from the body. People's hearts, as powerful transmitters, are constantly sending out electro-magnetic field waves. The physical antenna that is able to pick up these waves is the elaborate sensory apparatus of our whole body if the antenna is tuned in.[9]

Babies are very tuned in, as adults can be when truly present. Dee Coulter talks of a study with young children on a playground whose parents simply sat around the edge, not interfering with the children. A soccer field lay beyond the playground and the researchers had child friendly dogs and people walk toward the playground with no response from the children. However, when a convicted child molester walked toward the playground, though they neither saw nor heard this person, the children immediately left their play and went to their parents.[10] How did the children know there was a dangerous person present? The powerful vibration field around the heart makes it possible for us to be affected by or affect other people and may explain how these highly sensitive/receptive children were able to pick up another person's coherence or incoherence.[11, 12]

VIP—Our True Identity

Many scientists are seriously exploring the world beyond three-dimensional space and opening up the notion that we are much more than what we can see, touch, taste, smell and hear. They claim that our experiences emanate from sensations coming from a vast sea of available vibrations.

When I was teaching college biology I always began the course with the story of the Big Bang, leading my students through the formation of galaxies and stars and on to the eventual demise of those stars as they formed novas or supernovas. I would dramatically explain that from the intense temperatures and pressures of those dying stars, the elements (atoms) in the periodic table were formed. These were the same elements or atoms that made up our bodies and the structures of all animate and inanimate things on earth. I would always end by saying "We are children of the universe, connected to everything through atoms." The atom, believed to be the sacred icon on which all life was formed, became the basis for biology.

However, our understanding of the atom changed radically with the advent of particle accelerators that could split the atom and discover its secrets. The spaces within the atom are much greater than I could have imagined. For example: if the nucleus were the size of a typical California orange in San Francisco, the first orbital with its orbiting electrons, would be in Chicago. And in-between the nucleus and orbital there is SPACE, making our physical structure 99.9999% space. Dr. William Tiller, professor emeritus from Stanford, claims that space is a chaotic sea of boundless energy.[13] So physically we can think of ourselves as mostly boundless energy.

99.9999%
space

Figure 4.1: Atomic Model

You might take a look at yourself in a mirror right now and see the space in you, filled with energy, rather than the solid being we've learned to perceive. And then see others that way: it's a mind expander.

Using sophisticated particle accelerators, we now have enough beam energy to even take apart the electrons and nucleus of the atom only to discover that they aren't matter (particles) at all, but rather Vibrational Interference Patterns (VIPs). Fritjof Capra, physicist at Berkley, says *"Subatomic particles, and all matter made there from, including our cells, tissues, and bodies, are in fact patterns of activity rather than things."*[14]

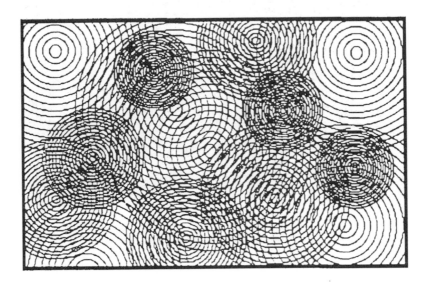

Figure 4.2: *Representation of Vibrational Interference Patterns*

The vibration pattern that makes up our structure would probably appear much like the circle pattern formed when we throw many rocks into a still pond. As the circles move out from the point of impact, they would overlap each other forming a pattern. Perhaps the places where they overlap, the interference·areas of the pattern, give us a perception of matter.

According to more current researchers, there really isn't matter, except as we perceive it within the context of our reality.[15] It is a fascinating exercise for me to make a paradigm exploding game out of seeing everyone and everything as vibrational patterns. It is like peering around the corner into another world, much like the picture in Figure 4.3.

Figure 4.3: Alternate Reality

*"Matter is nothing more than energy vibrating at frequency low
enough that we can perceive it with our senses."*
—*Albert Einstein*

The energy Einstein speaks about is measured as the vibrational
electromagnetic spectrum, which is enormous, spanning between
the slowest sound vibrations at less than 3 Hz (cycles/sec.) to cosmic rays at 10^{28} Hz (cycles/second). Figure 4.4 shows the complete
spectrum.

Beyond the Five Senses

We are vibrations existing in a sea of vibration. Our senses become the step-down transducers, which slow and break down the
vibrational continuum into tiny, discrete pieces that can be ana-
lyzed by our sensory receptors and reassembled into a pattern in

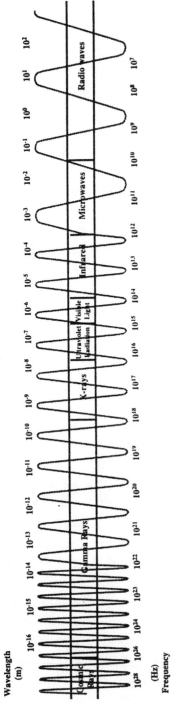

Figure 4.4: Electromagnetic Spectrum of Vibration

the brain, according to our paradigm.[16] There is no sound without the ear receiving it; otherwise it is just sound vibration.[17] The idea of only five senses and sensory receptors has been challenged by researchers R. Rivlin and K. Gravelle who have expanded them to include at least nineteen.[18] Figure 4.5 is a picture of Breeze picking up her sensory world using much more than just our believed five senses.

In Western society, we tend to lean heavily on our visual sense, "seeing is believing." However, only 4% of vision is light being received by the eye, the other 96% is manufactured in the brain according to our other senses and kinesthetic/emotional reality. We only perceive the spectrum of visible light through our adult vision, which sees what it expects to see and nothing more. Embryos, fetuses, newborns and young children seem to still be sensitive to a much larger part of the vibrational spectrum.

Many other cultures use a more open and integrated approach to their senses, highly developing all of them and, in the process, experiencing sensory input that adults in the West seldom experience. I had an interesting experience with an Indian woman named Amaige who spoke no English. I had gone to an open concert where she and her devotees were singing "bagans", beautiful and inspiring spiritual songs. At the end of her concert she invited people to come and greet her. When I finally reached her, she smiled, looked into my eyes, took my hands and I was flooded with the most amazing sensations I have ever felt. It was the sensation of coming home, of being absolutely loved, of being completely whole. I experienced magnetism between us, a power surge of energy, a full opening of all my senses and great joy.

The major power transfer of information that occurred between Amaige and myself required rugged and robust, energy-handling gear (trunk lines, etc.) to transport the information exchange. The heart, with its large coherent electro-magnetic field, fits that description. Her wonderfully coherent heart brought my alpha brain waves into synchrony, opening my system to experience all the rich array of vibrations available to me that I had been unaware of.[19] I certainly felt my heart, and hers, as she simply held my hands. The fact that I felt, even on the conscious level, all that electricity,

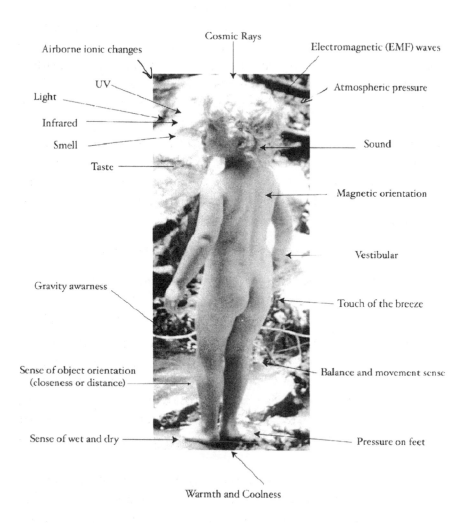

*Figure 4.5: Breeze Experiencing Her 19 Senses
as per Rivlin and Gravelle*

that broad spectrum of vibration, shows me it is always possible if we choose to be open and sensitive to it.

I believe we can consciously retrain our senses to be more available to all the rich vibrational fields when we honestly look with "child eyes" from our coherent hearts at our world and each other. A simple way to begin looking with "child eyes" is to stand up, lean over and look through your legs at the world—the image is astonishing and new. Everything in our world is always new—the vibrational patterns are constantly shifting, and in each moment, we are presented with a whole new set of pleasure sensations. Because of our training, we usually see what we expect to see, rather than the newness and reality I believe is such a part of the young child's world.

The Heart As Emotion Generator

"The heart is the source of our intuition which is eventually perceived at the brain/mind level."
—*Rollin McCraty*[20]

Multifunctional sensory nervous tissue throughout the heart is receptive to hormones, information peptides, and changes in pressure and nervous stimulation originating from within the heart.[21] It also responds to messages sent from the amygdala in the limbic system of the brain. The amygdala and its related structures are considered key emotional centers and storehouses for our emotional memories.

Our emotions, via the amygdala, tend to modulate our behavioral, immunological and neuroendocrine responses to threats. Our emotional memory, developed from past experience, colors our perception and determines how we will react or respond to current situations.[22] Beginning with sensory input, the brain monitors old memories looking for a match that might require survival tactics. If there is uncertainty or similarity with past events, the whole fight or flight response takes over. In a new relationship, our new friend may do something that triggers an emotional memory of a previous relationship. If the previous relationship was painful or frustrating, our amygdala will match that action to our new friend and lead us to assume this relationship will be the same. This fear causes us to react in a protective way, though the action of the new friend may and probably does have a completely different context. My problems with my husband, Jim, came from assumptions that dated back to the abandonment I felt from my father. The amygdala alerted me to watch for similar situations or actions from Jim, and sure enough, I saw and reacted to him as my father. No wonder misunderstandings occur.

But how we react/respond to our world doesn't begin with just the amygdala; it begins with the complex interplay between the *heart* and the amygdala. The heart sends a message of either coherence or incoherence to the amygdala that affects the emotions governing our thoughts and reactions.[23]

All of the information chemicals (neurotransmitters) found in the brain are also found in the heart.[24] The heart is also a hormonal gland, classified as such in 1983, releasing two major hormones that also affect the brain. The first hormone, ANF (Atrial Natriuretic Factor) affects many major organs of the body including the regions of the brain that regulate our emotional state and influence our learning and memory.[25] The second hormone, ICA (Intrinsic Cardiac Adrenergic) synthesizes and releases adrenalin and dopamine.[26, 27] Thus, the messages between the heart and brain exist as neurochemical, electrochemical or hormonal connections.

Current research[28] leads us to believe that the heart is constantly monitoring our entire environment, both inner and outer, and setting up a heart rate variability pattern that is either coherent or incoherent. This coherent or incoherent heart rate variability pattern is then relayed from the heart to the brain through the vagus nerve to the medulla oblongata, thalamus and amygdala. *There is more nervous information going from the heart to the brain than vice-versa.* At the same time, hormonal information from the heart is also affecting the brain.

Coherence/Incoherence—Viva La Difference

If the heart rate variability is coherent (as with a natural curious, focused learning state; peace; joy; appreciation; love; a sense of belonging; and creativity), the amygdala senses that good feeling and internally maintains normal heart rate, blood pressure and relaxed breathing via the parasympathetic nervous system. A coherent HRV pattern enhances the ability of the thalamus to easily take in all the sensory information from the environment (seeing, hearing, taste, touch, proprioception, etc.) thus setting an optimal state for learning.

The amygdala then stimulates the production of a coherent brain wave pattern in the basal part of the frontal lobes (prefrontal cortex), and the association area of the neo-cortex receives the information and brings it into full consciousness. Coherence allows the brain to easily take in all the diverse sensations from the environment, and put them into patterns that can be used by the brain to learn, remember, and expand understanding to create new ideas. This is the optimal state for learning.

"Human perception and learning arise from synchronized (coherent) activity of clusters of neurons in order to render unified scenes and meaning from diverse sensations."[29]

Eugenio Rodriques, et al.

If the heart frequencies are incoherent (as with any threat to our safety, or stress leading to frustration, anxiety, fear, worry and anger), the amygdala senses danger and the sympathetic nervous system and cortico-releasing factor (CRF) are triggered. Stress hormones (adrenalin, and cortisol) flood the system causing the person to react in a defensive, protective way to the situation. The thalamus shuts down to any sensory information not directly related to survival, thus decreasing our ability to take in all the rich sensory information of our environment for growth and learning.

An incoherent brain wave pattern is set up in the basal part of the frontal lobes and association area of the neo-cortex decreasing the brain's ability to combine information in patterns that lead to high-level reasoning, learning and creativity. The emotional memory of the event will be stored, but learning, aside from survival will be minimal.

The Heart/Brain Interface

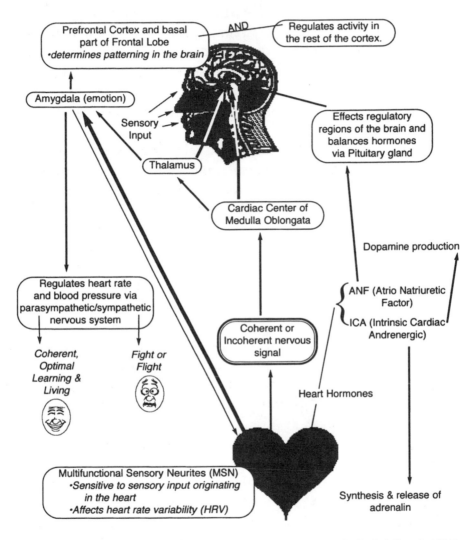

© 2000 Carla Hannaford, Ph.D.

Figure 4.6: The Heart/Brain Interface

This research has challenged me to rethink my whole life. Every event in my life is simply that, an event. How I perceive and act on these events is colored by the memory of my early experiences. Yet I always have a choice of how I experience each new event, though it may take conscious reprogramming. For instance, I can choose coherence during a traffic jam, using the extra time to look around, come up with new ideas, sing or just be still for a moment in my day. When I practice to develop coherence by consciously focusing on what is right in my life, take relaxing regular walks in nature, do slow integrated movements like yoga, Tai Chi, Chi Gong, or Brain Gym®, and connect to others from my heart, coherence becomes more spontaneous.

Because of the large electromagnetic field generated by our heart, we can actually affect the coherence/incoherence of another person by simply being close to them. Our brain picks up the heart fields of others. When several people are within six feet of each other and hooked up to EKG's, there is a measurable signal between one person's heart and the other person's brain. If the heart rate pattern of one person is coherent, the other person will synchronize with the first person's heart rate by exhibiting coherent alpha brain wave rhythms as measured by an EEG (electro-encephalogram).[30, 31]

When stress is chronic, incoherent brain wave patterns become the homeostatic state for people, the pattern they are most at home with. If they are put into a coherent situation, it often feels foreign to them, so they may "stir things up" until there is incoherence so they feel more at home.

I see this all the time in classrooms when children coming from incoherent, survival-oriented lives, don't know what to do with coherence. One incoherent child in the class has the potential to disturb the entire class. The teacher may be very coherent, so the child, in an attempt to feel what he usually experiences in his life, pushes until the teacher "loses it" and becomes incoherent, and then the child feels more at home. These are the children we tend to label hyperactive, attention deficit or emotionally handicapped. I also see it in people who thrive on "drama" in their lives.

The good news is: the strongest, most natural state is coherence, and we will gravitate back to that state if given the chance. I believe that is why there are certain people I love to be around. Just their presence brings me into coherence, and I am able to be more authentically myself with them. A wonderful instant coherence establisher/defense tactic is to do Hook Ups® while focusing on your breathing pattern or heart. I have used this technique in many situations and call it "making a heart connect". It can be used anywhere, home, office, school, in a traffic jam—anywhere. (See Hook Ups® description: Chapter 2, p. 20).

When someone is really suffering and can't pull themselves back into coherence, I stand close to them in Hook Ups® (within their heart field), and focus on my breathing and/or heartbeat. Within moments, they come back to that natural coherent state and relax. It works best when the children/adults initiate the "heart connect", and everyone does it. If the incoherent person is resistant, your coherence will still affect them.

I've learned that when all the kids in the classroom are "bouncing off the walls", I better check my level of coherence. I am almost always in an incoherent state and the students are just mirroring me. It's a great time for me to take a one minute "heart connect" to pull myself together again, and miraculously, the students settle down also. It is far more effective than yelling, scolding or penalizing. Children seem to realize the benefits and do it on their own when they start to feel out of control. When we are incoherent and out of control, we alienate other people, and isolate ourselves from the love and appreciation we all need. Children know this more keenly than we think.

The heart runs the show, acting as though it has a mind of it's own, profoundly affecting perception, intelligence and our interaction with others.[32] As parents, educators, and friends, we miss the boat by focusing on an agenda when the heart energy is not straightened out first.

The Problem With Thinking

Interestingly, thinking gets in the way of heart/brain coherence by taking us away from the moment and each other.[33] Thinking actually decreases blood flow to the heart and inhibits the normal functioning of a heart factor that brings the heart back into coherence, coined the "L" Factor by Dr. Paul Pearsall, psychologist.[34]

If we are totally in the present, relaxed and allowing our thoughts to just flow, ideas, understanding, and appropriate action occur naturally. The resulting coherence not only affects those around us, but can also affect inanimate objects. A study done at Princeton University illustrates this. Volunteers were asked to consciously attempt to alter the output of numbers from a random numbers generator. A random numbers generator is simply a computer that prints out numbers in a random way over a period of time. The study showed that if the volunteers concentrated on and thought hard about changing the output of numbers, it lessened their influence on the output of numbers. On the other hand, if volunteers set a simple intention to change the output of numbers and then just relaxed, their influence on altering the computer was greater.[35]

I have a knack for generating stress in that time right before dawn when its too cold to get out of bed and my wide awake brain seems to run out of control. Thoughts that bring up fear or worry or something I forgot to do cascade in, ruining my morning peace. If I have the presence to breathe and focus on the birds calling up the morning, I can stop the runaway thoughts; otherwise I enter the day incoherently.

Two cardiologists, Michael Cooper and Michael Agent, did an interesting experiment with a group of men who had very elevated cholesterol levels (ranging between 300 – 500). These men had been cardiac patients, some with severe problems. Besides keeping diet, exercise and body weight constant, these high risk men were trained to sit quietly for 15 minutes a day and clear their minds. They were told that if a fearful or worrisome thought came into their head, to just let it pass and come back to the present. Almost immediately, this caused the cholesterol levels to drop by one third. This kind of a drop is unheard of except with one specific drug now on the market. And this highly effective technique is cheaper and safer than any drug.[36]

When I first read that thinking inhibits coherence, I had a knee jerk reaction. Aren't we supposed to think? Isn't that the responsible intellectual thing to do, to figure out our whole life, to orchestrate every minute so we're safe in knowing what's coming next? Then I started "thinking" about it. In the times when I'm truly creative, I'm not thinking about or even trying to be creative. I'm just in the moment, and the most remarkable ideas come to me.

According to Harvard professor Mihalyi Czikszentmihalyi, creativity occurs from a playful, naïve place when there is no worry about failure, no self-consciousness, and no sense of time. He terms this being in the "Flow", a form of "in the moment stream of consciousness" that allows us to learn, to have new ideas and feelings about what we experience, thus assuring the "AHA" and creativity in our lives.[37]

In Traditional Chinese Medicine, the Heart and Mind are considered to be the same and felt to be affected by either excessive thinking or excessive emotional strain. The notion of "Not thinking too much nourishes the heart" is heavily influenced by Taoist ideas of "nourishing life" by calming the mind and preventing distracting thoughts.

THE YUM SOLUTION

STOP: Stop the run away thoughts on past and possible futures.

Be aware of where you are at this moment with no distractions.

Be present, with who you are and who others are at this moment.

Take long, slow breaths from your belly.

LOOK: Look at your world with child eyes, making it a totally new experience.

Look at yourself honestly as a valuable, unique being.

Look at others or the situation as the perfect learning situation.

LISTEN: Listen to the rich sounds of nature.

Listen from your heart to the tone of another's voice and words.

Listen to your intuition or gut feelings.

TOUCH: Reconnect through touch, it is our strongest anchor and bridge.

Hug yourself and others with the hug of the beloved.

Touch with your eyes, meeting another's eyes with total love.

In a difficult situation extend your hand, and turn with the other person to look at the situation *before* you instead of *between* you.

MOVE: Take a relaxed walk, swim or bike-ride, being aware of the feel, the smells, and the sights.

Relax your shoulders and open your heart.

Do Yoga, Tai Chi, Brain Gym,® or dance to your favorite music.

Move your mouth in song, laughter or praise of yourself and others.

YUM: With pleasure, recognize and bless who you are, what you have in your life and the people and situations that assist your growth.[38]

We don't need expensive technology, expensive therapies or designer drugs to come home to the heart. It only takes a moment of being truly present and coherent, to change the incoherence, not only in ourselves, but also in those around us. This forces us to more responsibly trust ourselves for the solutions, giving us back the power to structure our lives as we choose.[39,40]

CHAPTER FIVE

In the Beginning—Stress in Utero

"There is no period of parenthood with a more direct and formative effect on the child's developing brain than the nine months of pregnancy leading to the birth of a full term baby."
—*Marian Diamond* [1]

I see more and more pregnant women and parents living hurried, stress filled lives. Because of this, I am compelled to share what the research community has known for years, though it is finally reaching the popular press. If only I had known this when I was pregnant with Breeze, I would have been very grateful.

Hundreds of studies show the vulnerability of the unborn child, its sensitivity, impressionability and ability to relate to the mother's emotional state.[2, 3, 4] I am only now beginning to understand how deeply everything I felt as an uncertain newly married, pregnant professional woman influenced Breeze in those nine months that we shared my body. Every thought and action gave rise to hormones and other biochemicals that created a pleasurable or incoherent fetal environment for Breeze. She was influenced by my joy, my stress, loud sounds, movement, my heart beat, electro-magnetic fields, and even my thoughts, to name a few. Her entire world, the way she now perceives it, the way she adjusts to it, has been shaped, however minimally by what happened in the womb.[5,6]

I am astounded at the previously unimagined extent environmental influences play on the infinitely complex embryonic development. In the first month and a half of my pregnancy, as I was river rafting on the Colorado River, Breeze would have already been responding to touch. Touch in the womb influences the developing embryo in two important ways; it stimulates the development of the withdrawal reflex for survival and also stimulates physical development.

The withdrawal reflex develops at just 5 weeks after conception. If the embryo's upper lip touches something in her amniotic world, she will withdraw immediately in an amoeba-like response. Just days later, the palms of her hand, soles of her feet and eventually her whole body becomes responsive to touch.

Physical development in utero takes place as a reaction to the force of the mother's uterus and the amniotic fluid exerting pressure on the developing embryo. Already, the embryo has developed a sense of identity, of solidness through this touch in utero.[7] Touch is vital for development, with research showing that premature babies who are massaged get to go home 6 days earlier than babies who aren't.[8] Touch increases the release of nerve growth factor (NGF), which stimulates nerve development and strengthens the developing neurons so the child matures to a healthy, viable state faster.

It was almost instinctual for me to rub my belly, touch her through my skin and wrap my arms across her, not knowing I was exerting the pressure necessary for her to take material form. In subsequent work with children who are hypersensitive to touch and/or very hyperactive, I would have them roll up tightly in a blanket, which relaxed and calmed them almost immediately. The swaddling of these children, as with a newborn, helps to maintain their sense of solidness and identity.

By 9 weeks, the webbed fingers of the fetus have developed enough to wrap her palm around objects. By 12 weeks, she would be able to close her fingers and thumb in readiness for grabbing my finger, the first pleasure of touch we would share after birth.[9]

The withdrawal reflex lessens as an awareness of touch becomes familiar, and the Moro Reflex takes its place at about 9 weeks. The Moro or Startle Reflex is our earliest form of the "fight or flight" response. Even as adults, we still experience a modified version of the Moro Reflex when someone startles us unexpectedly. Our arms and legs jerk outward from the body accompanied by a sudden intake of breath; then with the exhale comes a scream.[10]

The Moro Reflex is naturally triggered after birth by loud sounds, sudden movements or, in some cases the removal of the secure blankets off a baby to change its diapers. The infant's screams and stiff thrown out arms and legs may act to scare off an intruder or to alert a caregiver to bring help. The Moro Reflex is usually inhibited by 2–3 months after birth, but can be seen longer, (as hyperactivity, hypersensitivity, lack of focus and autism) in babies and children whose mothers experienced chronic or traumatic stress during pregnancy.[11] Autistic children, as an extreme example, withdraw or run away screaming when a sudden sound, movement, light or change in balance occurs. These children remain stuck in survival.[12] Sally Goddard states, "While other residual reflexes tend to have an impact on specific skills, it is the Moro which has an overall effect on the emotional profile of the child."[13]

Dr. Lester W. Sontag, in studying pregnant women during WWII, was the first to make us aware of the effects of maternal anxiety on the fetus. During pregnancy, the effects of chronic stress, from elevated adrenalin and cortisol, are passed along to the fetus, with the outcome often being irritable babies who are hyperactive. The adrenalin from the mother increases the fetal heart rate while cortisol acts on the brain, preventing some of the dendritic branches and spines on the nerve cells from forming and cutting the number of neurons. This can affect ease of learning.[14] In chronically anxious mothers, the levels of hyperactivity in the fetus can be 10 times that of fetuses in relaxed mothers.[15] During amniocentesis in one study, when the mothers and fetuses were relaxed, the doctors told each mother that her baby was not moving. This immediately raised the anxiety of the mothers, and within seconds the fetuses were kicking furiously.[16] Babies with high stress in utero exhibit reduced resistance to disease, sleep and feeding disorders, and in extreme cases, as much as 60% delays in their normal development.[17,18,19,20,21]

Stress in pregnancy also leads to increased blood pressure, sending more blood to the mother's big muscles for fight or flight while shunting blood away from the developing baby. This lack of blood to the baby squeezes off as much as 60% of her oxygen and nutrient supply.[22,23]

The rhythm of the mother's heart, if coherent, sets up an early pattern for the developing brain, assisting the child later to organize the patterns of other vibration, such as language. Each language has a specific pattern/rhythm that must be learned in order to become linguistically proficient. When stressed, the mother's heart rate becomes irregular or incoherent, entraining that incoherent pattern on the fetus, which could make language and other learning more difficult later on. Music with a coherent pattern has the ability to establish a coherent heart rhythm in the pregnant mother and fetus, thus reducing hyperactivity in the fetus. Music also helps to decrease depression in pregnant mothers by bringing the heart back to coherence.[24]

Auditory conditioning and preferences after birth are influenced by what fetuses hear in utero.[25] For better or worse, my biology lectures and occasional singing with my guitar and/or violin playing helped make up Breeze's pre-natal repertoire. She is definitely a singer today, preferring the songs I sang during my pregnancy (Peter, Paul and Mary; Simon and Garfunkle, etc.) Similarly, Boris Brott experienced his mother's cello playing when she was pregnant with him. Now, as the conductor of the Hamilton Ontario Philharmonic Symphony, he is able to easily pick out cello parts without knowing them when conducting the same pieces his mother played before his birth.[26]

In a wondrous study where pregnant mothers read *The Cat in the Hat* to their fetuses 2 times a day for 6½ weeks, the newborns would suck enthusiastically when they heard mom's voice reading *The Cat in the Hat* piped through a plastic nipple, compared to her reading another story.[27]

According to researchers, in the last three months of my pregnancy, as I was finishing up the quarter at the college and feeling enormous but energetic, Breeze was exhibiting REM sleep, believed to allow her to rehearse movements she could not do in the womb because it was too crowded. Also her powers of recall would be well developed, especially for sounds, survival situations and my emotional states.[28]

A mother's attitude appears to have the single greatest effect on how an infant will turn out.[29] Breeze represented a second chance for me to fully embrace being a parent, to somehow make up for the child I gave up for adoption, and I was very grateful for this new life developing in mine. For many women, an unexpected pregnancy carries less positive feelings. Any conflict, ambivalence, or rejection the mother feels in relation to her unborn child can be reflected in the fetus's increased activity and difficulties throughout life related to having been prenatally unwanted.[30,31,32] Additionally, an unexpected pregnancy can leave a women depressed, feeling out of control of her life with that incoherence extending to the fetus and child. In a study on depressed mothers, a high percentage of infants had been hyperactive in utero, and twice the number as compared to wanted children became late or poor walkers.[33]

EMF's in Utero

Besides maternal stress, another stress impacting the embryo and fetus is the electro-magnetic field (EMF) of the mother's environment, easily conducted through the amniotic sac. This EMF bombards us from electric kitchens, microwave ovens, irons, vacuums, hair dryers, TVs, computers, cell phones, transit systems (trains, cars, planes), fluorescent lights, etc. The electro-magnetic field in our current environment is said to be 300 times greater than what our grandparents had to deal with as they were growing up. These sensitive embryos, fetuses, and children, acutely aware of everything, are being so over-stimulated that they remain in survival mode—ALL THE TIME.

Dr. Dee Coulter cites research showing that more newborns in technologically advanced cultures are exhibiting an "excited" state—almost a state of shock at birth. They lack the natural rhythm for rocking and sucking coordination that in previous generations was established in the womb.[34] Recently, an occupational therapist working with newborns shared with me the fact that more and more newborns are having difficulty nursing because they can't establish the complex rhythm and sequence necessary to suck. The influence of EMF interference and mother's stress during pregnancy gave her some possible causes.

Stanford University chemists noted the ability of low frequency EMF's to disrupt lipid membranes such as those that serve as the gatekeepers for chemicals entering or exiting our cells. This would affect cellular functions in a developing embryo/fetus and also the infant/child's learning skills which are dependent on proper functioning of the nervous system at the cellular level.[35]

Early Trauma

Life experiences beginning in utero, shape the wiring patterns in the brain and set our sensitivity levels to stress. Early trauma can affect all of the following:

1. neural development in the pre-frontal cortex (PFC), leading to chronic over secretion of adrenalin and cortisol and high sensitivity to stress;

2. a loss of glial cells that stabilize the levels of glutamate, a neurotransmitter that activates nerve cells (With more glutamate, there is over-stimulation of neurons that moderate negative emotions to the amygdala. This over-stimulation causes these neurons to burn out (collapse and shrink) so no message is sent to the amygdala to decrease the negative emotions and stress reaction. This leads to an over-reactive system with no modulation.[36]);

3. a decrease in the levels of BDNF (brain derived neurotrophic factor), a specific nerve growth factor which strengthens the connections in the hippocampus and enhances the growth of neurons that respond to seratonin (This causes nerve cell growth to be suppressed in parts of the hippocampus that are capable of renewing nerve cells in adult life. Therefore, a lifelong pattern of brain activity becomes established that produces an exaggerated response to stress, leaving the body at a loss to adapt appropriately.[37,38]); and

4. an increase in early adverse life events which have the potential to create adult psychopathology.

This frightens me considering the stress I was under during my pregnancy. However, one thing is certain: our human system is highly plastic and repairable given the proper tools and time. These tools must include the pleasures of heart connection, touch, movement and play.

Brain Development Results

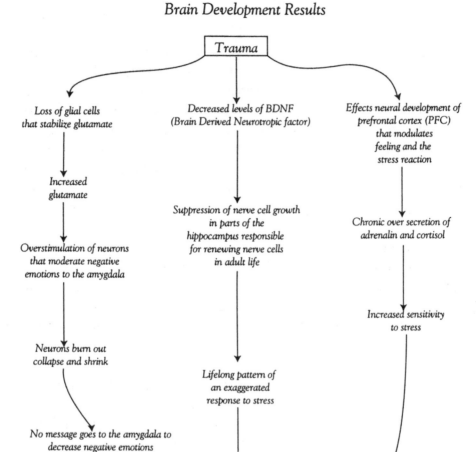

Figure 5.1: *Trauma/stress and brain adaptation*

I like that besides the doses of adrenalin and cortisol I dished out, Breeze also received large quantities of interlukins and interferons, information molecules produced when I was joyful. She might even have enjoyed our ski trips when I was 5 to 7 months pregnant with her. Since I had learned to ski in powder snow, I could never get my weight forward on my skis to accommodate the icy slopes of Colorado—that is until Breeze was my belly partner. As a team we had a great forward lean, and I know she experienced the same delight and joy I did at the exhilaration of our fast, graceful, controlled movements down the beautiful Colorado mountainside. Her recall and REM sleep for practicing the movements may have been why she seemed to be a natural born skier when she first took to the slopes.

"Natural born" is an interesting phrase that makes sense applied to children with special abilities who may have gained these abilities in utero. It certainly would apply to Mozart, who must have been surrounded by a sea of music during his pre-natal experience. It is the coherent vibrations that increase the learning experience—as in the pleasure I felt at the joy of skiing and that Mozart's mother must have felt with music.

In many cultures worldwide, pregnancy has been a time of conscious relaxation and joy for the mother. In Bali, when women discover they are pregnant, they immediately start telling the unborn child stories of the various Hindu Gods, singing, and welcoming the child in every way. The mother tells the unborn child about the wonders of the world it is about to enter and all about the family that will embrace it. She feels she must find joy in everything she does so the child will also be a joyful child. During my time in Bali, I never saw a hyperactive Balinese child. These cultures have lived in a way maximally conducive to healthy, bright, joyful children. Because they are so in tune with their developing children, they practice haptonomy, the ability to communicate spontaneous empathy through their thoughts. This nurtures and protects the embryo and fetus.[39]

Parenting the Unborn and Newly Born

The strength and quality of the fundamental cord of love spun between mother and child determines the whole vast tapestry of human relationships: person-to-person, person to society, person to the environment, and ultimately our global connection. It stems from the early, in utero, and birth bonding. Here are some ideas on how to assure the health of that bonding:

During Pregnancy:

1. Experience as much pleasure, tranquility, heart patterned music, laughter, and physical activity as possible. Women that burn 1,000 to 2,000 calories/week in pleasant recreational activities deliver babies weighing 5% to 10% more than inactive women and the babies are able to weather physical adversity better.[40]
2. Practice good stress management skills that ensure mental and emotional freedom from fear. Doctors should be very careful not to use intimidating medical terms that might frighten the expectant mother or language that anticipates problems.
3. Welcome the developing embryo and fetus into your thoughts, sharing heart to heart talks, stories, music and laughter.
4. Eat good wholesome balanced food, rich in essential amino and fatty acids, breathe fresh air, and drink lots of water.

To Facilitate a Gentle Birth:

1. Hospital delivery should be the exception, not the norm. Be properly prepared for a natural childbirth with good professional backup and a supportive birthing coach. Remain as calm and relaxed as possible. A pleasant home environment helps.
2. Natural birth without drugs or anesthesia allows both the mother and baby to be fully present for maximum bonding. Odors produced by the fetus actually alter the odor of the mother, allowing the mother to identify her child at birth and vice-versa—an important factor in parent-infant bonding.[41] Drugs could inhibit that process.
3. During delivery, the mother secretes large quantities of oxytocin that assists the birth process as well as maternal bonding

behavior. Both baby and mom will have produced endorphins, which reduce pain, and intensify a state of dependency.[42] The first hour after the birth is critical for bonding. The mother and baby will be attracted to each other's dilated pupils and should be together, uninterrupted as the oxytocin levels rise and the bonding process occurs. The father then holds the baby and his oxytocin rises, assuring bonding. (This can be repaired later but only with great effort and determination.)

4. The new baby needs as much cuddling as possible to stimulate all the senses and establish a sense of safety. Touch is essential, immediately assisting the newborn to organize sensory input into coherent information and respond with action. Without touch, the child may survive but can be seriously dysfunctional.[43] If nerve endings aren't activated, the reticular formation in the brain will not be fully operative, leading to impaired movements, curtailed sensory intake, and a variety of emotional disturbances and learning problems.[44]

5. Breast-feeding releases endorphins in both the mother and baby, blocking the pain of delivery and relaxing them both. The high tryptophane content of mother's milk produces serotonin in the baby, which helps to regulate a calm mood, induce a calm sleep, and assist in the newborn optimally taking in sensory information for learning. Mother's milk also enhances antibodies and many infection fighting agents in the baby.[45,46,47,48]

6. It is optimal for the baby to stay with the mother and for the parents/caregivers to immediately answer any cries from the baby with secure close touch and a reassuring voice.[49]

I wonder about the baby I gave up for adoption, the baby that had grown in me for 9 months, whom I felt such a deep love and attachment with. I think about how she had been yanked from me at birth, no time for even a hug, no touch to soften the separation or grieving process for either of us. I wonder if that baby, now an adult, has been able to heal the wounds that initial brutal separation must have created, the wounds I still feel. Those first moments of life are so crucial to the sense of safety we all carry throughout our lives.

Breeze's birth came on a morning following the eclipse of the full moon. Her hospital birth was carefully orchestrated with low lights, quiet sounds, caring doctors and Jim. He held her almost immediately and I nursed and bonded with her for the hour following delivery. She was taken away from me while they took her vital signs and then not separated from me again. Breeze was the most beautiful being I had ever seen.

I loved our closeness, the quiet times nursing her, being oblivious to the rest of the world and so much in love with this tiny person. Unaware of the developmental implications. I remember those days as the most joyful, peaceful moments of my life. The closeness and play of those early years, even with the periodic separations of my teaching schedule, gave Breeze the template she needed to pull through the later stresses. And yet, perhaps the prenatal stress she had endured may have caused delays in developing certain reflexes and the steady beat patterning necessary to see and reproduce the linear patterns in reading and math that she struggled with later in school.

There is one constant in raising children: they will do what we do, not necessarily what we say. If we are stressed, they will also be stressed. Until about 15 months after birth, children see themselves as us, reflecting us back to ourselves. When our children are hyperactive or withdrawn, it could be our fear and frustration they are picking up. Parents remain the most significant people in children's lives, until ages 14 or 15 when they more fully embrace their peer culture.[50]

If we dare to look at our current lifestyles, especially when pregnant, parenting, or grandparenting, we begin to understand some of the underlying factors our children face. By maintaining ourselves in a more coherent way, we give our children clear models to access their own natural coherence.

Our children with their great sensitivity are like canaries in the mines, when it comes to reflecting our stress. Every individual, particularly those who have or will have children of their own, is responsible for co-creating the society of the future. That special period between gestation and early infancy determines the direction our society will take as well as the health of its members. "Instead of paying vast sums to fight the fires of escalating disease, learning disabilities, crime and violence, we could focus on the PREVENTION of these conditions by ensuring harmonious and nurturing uterine conditions for our future population."[51]

PRAYER OF THE UNCONCEIVED

"Men and women who are on Earth,
You are our creators.
We, the unconceived, beseech you:
Let us have living bread,
the builder of our new body.
Let us have pure water,
the vitalizer of our blood.
Let us have clean air
so that every breath is a caress.
Let us feel the petals of jasmine and roses
which are as tender as our skin.
Men and women who are on Earth,
you are our creators.
We, the unconceived, beseech you:
Do not give us a world of rage and fear,
for our minds will be rage and fear.
Do not give us violence and pollution,
for our bodies will be disease and abomination.
Let us be wherever we are rather than bringing us into
a tormented self-destroying humanity.
Men and women who are on Earth,
you are our creators.
We, the unconceived, beseech you:
If you are ready to love and to be loved,
invite us to this Earth of the thousand wonders.
And we will be born to love and to be loved."

—Laura Archera Huxley[52]

CHAPTER SIX

The Shapes of Our Reality

*"The only reason we're different is because of different experiences.
These create the software of our souls."*[1]
—Deepak Chopra

Breeze, this miracle that has so blessed my life, even as a newborn was far more than she initially appeared to be. Born to me, was this exquisite being, so small, so fragile, and so sensitively aware. In her beautiful perfection, she was like an alien exploring a new planet, alert and fascinated by everything.

I observed in awe as she explored new sounds, different and crisper than the sounds of her former watery environment. She listened intently to our voices, those of the dogs and cats who shared her home, the birds of spring and summer that gathered in the ancient trees around our home, the new voices of friends and grandma, the cacophony of traffic, sirens, airplanes, and children playing next door.

She welcomed the rich vibrant array of smells, carried through her now airy environment, from fresh spring flowers, next door's dinner, rain, furry animals exploring close to her nose, and the external scent of joy, frustration and love. She remembered my smell as she nursed on milk, spiced with my recent meal, while we rocked in the big rocking chair, undisturbed by time, space or other beings.

Her undeveloped eyes perceived brilliant new light patterns, scattered through the vaporous prism of morning dew to present her with light in all its visible and invisible forms. She elegantly sensed the light radiating from objects and people that swam as vibrational waves across her visual field.

Her now unbounded limbs experienced space and the touch of admirers who stroked and prodded her hands, face and feet, welcoming her to the outside world. She received a good dose of movement and touch during family baths and jostling in the baby carrier that held her close to my heart.

The shaping of her reality came from a combination of nature (genetics) and nurture (experience), though I am beginning to believe that experience is more profound than, and can override, genetics. All these experiences she absorbed with her highly sensitive system, perfectly designed to take in everything and learn at warp speed. She was acutely aware of sensations (vibrations), which I had long ignored or forgotten to be aware of.

The magnitude of this person, born into my care (sans owners manual) brought up all the fears (that every parent experiences) around my inadequacy to support her highest development. As all parents do, I chose to subject her to experiences that I felt would make her happy, brilliant, secure, and able to fit into the paradigms of the society I brought her into. As Breeze voraciously took in all the sensations of her world, I was unconsciously shaping which ones she would make a part of her reality.

People like Peter Russell and William Tiller are now defining consciousness as our ability to have experiences.[2] The nervous system, including the brain, may only be the amplifier of that consciousness, rather than its creator. The entire range of sensations bombards the developing embryo and fetus in a fairly random, chaotic manner. However, as the unborn child cues into (amplifies) the mother's patterns, the pressure of the mother's body, the mother's heartbeat, and the chemicals delivered from the mother, the child's perceptual world begins to take on some structure and order.

After the child is born, her world starts to be shaped by a whole new array of experiences. These physical/sensory experiences further structure the physical, mental and emotional perceptions that will determine which experiences she will be attracted to.[3]

"Thought requires a body—not in a trivial sense that you need a physical brain to think with, but in the profound sense that the way we structure our thoughts come from the nature of the body. Nearly all of our unconscious metaphors are based on common bodily experiences."[4]

—*George Lakoff and Mark Johnson*

We are all humans on this same home planet, and yet we are so different. Even identical twins have some differences. Mom, now 96, was raised in a family of eight, on a farm with no electricity, phone or motorized vehicles (until later). She has experienced vast changes in her life giving her a reality very different from mine as a post-war baby boomer or Breeze's as a child of the 70's and 80's.

Conditioning Our Reality

Unborn humans start with full awareness, sensitivity, and connection with all potentiality. As adults, our dogma, belief systems, habits, and life experiences narrow our connections with our true nature, and we have a hard time seeing beyond our perceived material world or our learned judgments.

For an understanding of how this narrowing occurs, it only takes looking at our own beliefs, habits, language and physiology. Below is a list of experiences that help determine our reality. For each item you might want to list how it has developed your belief system, habits, use of language, and your physiology:

» Being male or female
» Place in family of origin
» Main caregivers
» Race
» Specific family beliefs and emphases
» Location (urban/rural)
» Societal beliefs (family/tribe)
» Country of childhood
» Religion or spiritual beliefs
» Early education
» Labels (brilliant, dumb, gifted, smart, handicapped, etc.)
» Advanced education
» Cultural involvements (art, music, dance, sports, etc.)
» Media (T.V., news, magazines, journals, computers)
» Profession
» Status in profession
» Unemployment

- » Current economic status
- » Marital status
- » Adult labels (hippie, yuppie, senior citizen, new age, red neck)
- » Current age
- » Travel or contact with other cultures

All of these things and many more have formulated how we perceive our world and ourselves. We tend to gravitate towards experiences that fit our cultural belief system. For example: science tells us we are actually vibrational interference patterns—energy packets, connected with, influenced by, and influencing everything in a state of all possibilities. See Figure 6.1.

And yet, in our culture, we depend heavily on seeing to orchestrate our worldview and see ourselves as separate, physical, and immutable. The eye of the embryo, fetus, and newborn is taking in light as a pure vibration or waveform. She probably experiences her parents as a sensation of full spectrum radiant light, devoid of structure, and unmodified by any conditioning. Seeing the material world as our culture define it, with full acuity, color vision, and binocularity takes over a year after birth to develop.

We condition a baby's vision with solid objects from our material reality. The visual system is in large part set up by bodily kinesthetic information. Babies only begin to perceive components of their world as "objects" in those that move as a coherent unit (i.e., Mom), due either to real motion of the object relative to the background or to the motion of the infant.[5]

The vestibular system that controls how the eyes will move is tied directly into the core muscles that move the child into various positions, making the child able to explore her environment. This same system gives her a sense of object space and density in regards to gravity. All the various touch receptors, especially in her hands and lips, give her the sensations that shape how objects will become stored in visual memory. With a huge part of the sensory and motor cortices in the brain involved with the hand, the hand shapes our cognitive, emotional, linguistic and psychological development. Early childhood experiences of reaching and grasping determine

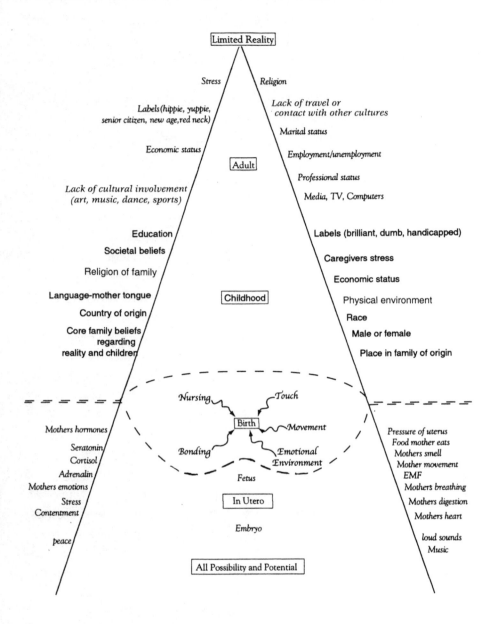

Figure 6.1: What impacts and determines our reality.

how the baby's brain will develop and how it will perceive its world.[6]

Through these physical/sensory experiences we unconsciously orchestrate her vision to focus and organize light in a particular way, according to our belief in the physical world. Only 4% of vision comes as light through the eye; the other 96% is manufactured in the brain from our experiences, which takes 1/5 of a second to process, so we don't actually get visual reality first hand (instantly).[7,8,9]

Slater demonstrated the illusion of vision in a 1930's experiment with upside down glasses. Experimental subjects were asked to continually wear glasses that turned their vision upside down and backwards. It took about two weeks to get past tripping over their environment, until their brains finally made the internal structural change, so they saw things "right side up". What they saw then appeared normal until they took the glasses off, and again, it took some time for their brains to right the image.[10]

Many people in Eastern cultures naturally see light vibrations that are emitted from other people—called auras. These people have maintained their sensitivity to light vibrations beyond the visible spectrum of our learned reality. They show us the potential is there if we can get past seeing what we expect to see based on our conditioned reality.

"We are led to believe a lie when we see with our eyes".
—*William Blake*

Our native language also conditions our reality. It was discovered that the Japanese brain is actually quite different from Western brains in where and how linguistic information is processed. The Japanese traditionally have a need to be immersed in natural sounds, such as bird and insect songs, animal cries, snow thudding off tree branches, ocean waves, and the wind in the forest. Their traditional life style, including their language, is based on a deep appreciation and harmony with nature and the environment and is, therefore, more dependent on the right hemisphere than Western societies, which rely more on the left hemisphere.[11,12] The implications here are that the very structure of the brain is influenced by our actual experiences of the world.[13]

Newborns and young babies have the ability to distinguish the sounds of all languages on the earth. But over time, the baby adopts the sounds it hears most frequently. A Japanese baby born in Japan will be unable to distinguish between "l" and "r" when she begins to speak, at about 9 months of age, and throughout her life.[14] However, if that Japanese baby were born in Hawaii and living in the midst of non-Japanese-speaking people, she would be able to distinguish between "l" and "r" and easily say "r" throughout her life. Thus, language is more a matter of experience than a physical trait.

Human Malleability

According to Ilya Prigogine, Nobel Prize winner, as living systems we are able to maintain our material existence because we are in essence a flexible, open energy system, which remains far from equilibrium.[15] We have the flexibility and potential to change our material structure depending upon the energy focused upon parts of that structure. What we truly put our attention on is processed internally, causing us to change our nerve networks, rework our memory, and actually change our brain and mind.[16]

The Japanese language focuses its energy pattern on the developing child, actually changing the structure of her brain and how she will structure her reality—in this case with a strong emphasis on nature. The malleability of our system and the choices we make to intentionally focus energy in certain ways may explain how we can change our physical, mental, and emotional reality throughout our lives.

Children are the most malleable, still tuned into most vibrations until we give them the message that it's not OK to have "imaginary playmates" or see things we don't see anymore. Then they shut down their sensitivity and only take in what will provide them approval. Approval is the strongest anchor of behavior, and pressures are great to fit in. It doesn't take much to start limiting the possibilities and block out much of the vibrational field available.

In Plato's *Republic*, he says our senses allow us to see only the shadows of ourselves, projected on the cave wall by fire light. But they inhibit us from seeing the actual being making the shadows—our true self, our full energetic, vibrational potential. To expand our current sensory awareness, we can practice seeing everything and everyone as vibrational patterns, full of all potential, with our heart instead of our head. Go back to the baby state, before the awareness of distinction, and separation, and reestablish consciousness without content, moving past limited vision to insight or inner sight from the heart.[17]

"Time and space are but the physiological colors that the eye makes, but the soul is light."
—*Ralph Waldo Emerson*

The Unified Information Field

To delve deeper into what constructs reality, let's look at the idea of a unified information field of vibration that we are all part of and can draw upon and affect. This field could be one way of explaining how embryos, fetuses and young children so easily pick up the world around them and learn at break-neck speed. It would also explain a phenomenon I often observed when Breeze was three and four years old. Out of the blue she would say, "Mommy, the phone is ringing, and it's Mary (or someone else)". THEN the phone would ring, and it would be Mary (or whomever she had said). She was somehow picking up energy patterns, vibrational information before they became material reality.

The same thing occurred between Mom and I at times when I was going through an emotional trauma in my life. I was usually at least 1,000 miles away from Mom and out of contact with her when a trauma would hit. Amazingly, she would call me at exactly the time I needed her, because she could somehow sense I was upset. Larry Dossey, M.D. elaborates on this phenomenon, which apparently occurs quite often between people who are emotionally close.[18]

To understand the concept of a unified information field, William Tiller and other scientists have shown that besides direct space/time (the material world), there also exists its antithesis—the vacuum, or reciprocal space/time. According to Tiller, reciprocal space/time consists of vibrational energy fields that exist within and beyond our physical body, subtly impacting and connecting us vibrationally to everything else.[19] It may be the field that underlies and organizes all the vibrational patterns that we experience as physical reality.

Light has always been a big anomaly for physicists, because relative to the observer, light always moves at the same speed. If you were traveling at almost the speed of light, light would still be traveling at 186,000 miles/second faster than you. Therefore, light doesn't experience time, space or matter, and Einstein attempted to explain this anomaly with his theory of Relativity. Because the behavior of light didn't make sense in direct space/time, it gave physicists a window into the possibility of a reciprocal reality.

In Einstein's equation: $E = MC^2$, nothing can travel faster than the speed of light. Einstein came to this conclusion because he demonstrated that as a particle approached light velocity, its mass would phenomenally increase, requiring extremely large (unattainable) amounts of energy to keep accelerating the particle, so that, in theory, it could never reach the speed of light. This theory missed the possibility of faster than the speed of light (supraliminal) movement in a unified field.

Mathematicians however, were able to design an equation that would justify supraliminal movement, called the Tiller Modification to $E = MC^2$.

This modification allowed for the development of equations, which mathematically described a Tachion (faster than light) domain in reciprocal space, which would help to explain the ESP (extra-sensory perception) between my Mother and I.[20]

Reciprocal space, where vibrations/information can travel faster than the speed of light, explains the phenomena of non-locality (things occurring in two or more places at the same time) and a unified (interconnected) information field. The experimental proof for this came from research around the EPR (Einstein, Podolsky, Rosen) Paradox of 1935 which claimed that changing a particle in one part of the universe would change a like particle in another part of the universe. In the experiment, if two particles had previously interacted (particles within an atom for example), no matter where they were in the universe, if one changed, the other would instantly change also. This has been verified with atomic studies.[21]

In this model, the quantum field is not located in a given region of space and time. What happens in one region instantaneously influences what occurs in another region without any energy being exchanged between the two regions. Interesting experiments done by Amit Goswani with meditators nicely illustrates the EPR Paradox. People that had meditated together were separated by a large distance (often over 2,000 miles) and hooked up to EEG (electroencephalogram) machines. One of the meditators was rigged with an apparatus that would flash a red light in their eyes. Whenever the light flashed in the meditator's eyes, the EEG pattern would change, and at exactly the same moment, the other meditator's EEG pattern would also change in exactly the same way.[22]

Reciprocal space, with its non-local, unified information field may explain why fetuses and very young children are so attuned to their mother's emotions and the world. Their understanding of the world may come first from reciprocal space, the realm of information, before it is recognized in material space/time. When our minds are elsewhere, where are they? Whenever we use our imaginations, we are leaving our current established reality behind for a time, to explore other possibilities. It is like hooking into the Internet with all its possibilities, and with what we find there, we can choose to change our software, our reality.

For thousands of years Eastern cultures have tended to be more aware of reciprocal space. A. Shearer, a yogic scholar may be referring to reciprocal space in his expression: "Deep within the mind, beyond the faintest flicker of thought, it (*our true nature*) is experienced as an undying and omnipresent vastness. It is absolute consciousness. The nature of life is to grow towards an ever more perfect and joyous expression of itself. Each living being has a nervous system, no matter how rudimentary. This acts as a localized reflector of the all-pervading consciousness, just as a mirror reflects light."[23]

Field Consciousness in Action

Psychokinesis is the word used for the mind reaching out across space to affect the behavior of matter in whatever form. Besides being impacted by the collective field, it appears we can also impact the field through our thoughts. Double blind studies, where half of a large group of heart attack patients were prayed for give us insight into psycho-kinesis. The people praying for these patients were given only first names, and the doctors, nurses, patients, or their families knew nothing of the experiment. The patients who were prayed for fared statistically much better than patients who were not prayed for.[24]

Another fascinating study was done by psychologist Roger Nelson at Princeton University's PEAR laboratory and replicated by psychologist Dick Bierman at the University of Amsterdam. They decided to find out if collective consciousness (people mentally focused on the same thing) could affect the pattern of an inanimate object. The researchers programmed a computer that generated random numbers (either 0 or 1) called a random numbers generator (RNG), to generate 400 random bits (either 0s or 1s) every six seconds. Each 400 bits were called a sample. Each RNG was programmed to collect samples for an hour before an event, during the event and for an hour after the event. The before and after data were considered the control samples. The number of 1's (ones) produced in 400 random bits was used to measure the degree of statistical randomness in the electronic circuit every six seconds.

They then measured 4 events: a Holotrophic Breath workshop (breathing with music for nine hours with 12 people); the March 27, 1995, Academy Awards Ceremony (televised to an estimated one billion people in 120 countries); the O.J. Simpson verdict on October 3, 1995 (to an estimated half-billion people worldwide via TV or Radio); and the July 1996 Olympic Ceremonies. In every case a most remarkable thing happened: In the Holotrophic Breath workshop, as the intense coherent attention of the group increased over the nine hours, the odds against randomness rose to about one thousand to one by the end of the workshop. In other words, the random numbers generator was no longer randomly putting out numbers. It had been affected somehow by the consciousness of the people and was now putting out the number 1 one thousand times for every time it put out a single 0.

With the Academy Awards, the researcher had one RNG 20 meters away from where he watched the broadcast and another 12 miles away at his laboratory. Both readings showed an unexpected degree of order during the periods of high audience interest—again, the odds against randomness being as high as 700 to one. In the O.J. Simpson verdict, the researchers used 5 RNGs (one at Princeton, one in Amsterdam and 3 in the laboratories in Nevada). Precisely when the court reporter read the verdict, all five RNGs suddenly peaked to their highest point in the two hours of recorded data, giving odds against randomness at approximately 800 to one.[25]

The implications of this are profound if we consider that our media is orchestrating how we view reality which in turn affects our collective information field. All of our media affects the way we experience the world, but TV is especially potent. By the mid 1970's, when Breeze was born, ninety-nine percent of homes in America had at least one TV, running 6 hours per day in an average household and 8 hours per day in households with children. Currently, children in the U.S. have watched 5,000 – 6,000 hours of TV per year before the age of five.[26]

Through TV, we are ingesting images that have been edited, cut, rearranged, sped up, slowed down, and sensationalized in hundreds of ways. Instead of direct experience, we are substituting a secondary version, full of confusion, fear and violence.[27,28] This incoherence determines our take on reality and affects our input into the collective unconscious, thus spawning drug or people abuse, crime, terrorism, armed-conflict, etc.[29] Through coherent consciousness and intention, we can also change the collective unconscious.

William Tiller and associates have shown us the power of coherent intentions on inanimate and animate systems. In experiments, a specific intention for a particular outcome was imprinted onto a simple electronic device using the pooled intentions of four highly qualified meditators. This device, along with a control device, was shipped to a laboratory 2,000 miles away. Because the focused intention was made to act as a true thermodynamic potential, the imprinted device overwhelmingly affected the intended responses. The key was the robust belief of the meditators who were tying into the unified information field with their intentions.[30] Our intentions determine our reality, giving us the ability to coherently, passionately live our lives as an adventure or become stuck in fear.[31]

In his new book, Tiller makes a bold claim: "human consciousness contributes to the creation and direction of the universe."[32] With evidence of a unified information field existing in reciprocal space, we may indeed be "Children of the Universe".

I am now more consciously aware that every thought governing my actions is not caged and housed only in my head. It is actually a missile, launched from my whole being into the non-local information field, that affects at some level everything around me. I am especially aware of being "picked up" by unborn and young children before they learn to tune me out, picked up by their elaborate sensing apparatus and stepped down into every cell of their body. Picked up are the vibrations of my thoughts, emotions, and judgments that govern my perceptions of the world.

My perceptions were manufactured over more than 50 years by the belief systems of my parents, culture, society, school, religion, gender, and race. My every experience shaped the elaborate synthesis of my sensual world into a contextual reality in consensus with my culture. I formulated a belief system of separateness, linearity, and myself as a body, connected only through experience to my family, society and the world.

But these children, unborn or newly born, are still unformed, unbounded, open to all vibrational patterns. They are alert to everything I project, sensitive to the survival value of each input, pulling together their reality in conjunction with my limited worldview. I must be very careful in the presence of these sensitives, careful not to limit their possibilities or stop their exploration due to my own fears and beliefs. I must be authentic, coherent, integrated, and also unbounded around them so they will not be caged by my dogma. These wondrous beings have the potential to show me an expanded, brighter world, one again full of all the vibrations I have blocked out.

The immense potential of the non-local, collective field of consciousness makes me rethink every aspect of my reality. I no longer see the world, or myself, as a flat two-dimensional canvas. I've moved beyond a three-dimensional linear, brain-oriented system, compelled by reasoning to view my world as matter, where I miss all the wondrous possibilities of being my mature wisdom and child wonder at the same time.[33]

"Minds deal with eternity, brains deal only with temporality."
—Buckminster Fuller

Storage of Our Reality

Just how our experiences become memory, as a basis for our reality, is still not fully understood. Memory is part of the 99.99% of us that is below the level of consciousness.[34] With all the incoming information (over forty thousand bits per second), a built-in "reality filter" (the Reticular Activating System in the brain stem) monitors the strength and nature of the sensory impulses and, in just milliseconds, uses the individual's current reality to determine the degree of importance."[35]

Further sifting in short-term memory, discards it, or sends it on to the hippocampus. The hippocampus consults the "emotional references" in the amygdala to determine if the information is worth long-term storage in the neo-cortex of the brain.[36] This information then either strengthens, reforms, or dissolves nerve networks to establish stronger, weaker, or different electrical patterns.

In this model, we've focused on the brain's role in processing memory, but we are discovering an intricate memory in the heart, which Gary Schwartz calls "Systemic Memory".[37] Paul Pearsall, a psychiatrist working with heart transplant patients, wrote about this memory in his book *The Heart's Code*. Following heart transplants, new heart recipients and their cardiologists report new likes and dislikes of everything, from use of words to food and clothing. They also noticed personality changes with recipients taking on some of the behaviors, and cravings of the people whose hearts they had received.[38]

Karl Lashley, working with rats in the 1940's, destroyed parts of their brains, yet found that they could still remember and react. He concluded that though certain limited regions of the nervous system *may be essential for retention, learning and retrieval memory is distributed through the body/mind system as a hologram.*[39,40]

The hologram, invented by Dennis Gabor in 1947 records the vibrational interference patterns of an object subjected to focused light. In making a hologram, a single laser beam is sent through a beam splitter, which creates two beams. One of the beams becomes the reference beam and is deflected by a mirror, through a diffusing lens which diffuses its rays, to fall upon an unexposed photographic plate. The second beam is also sent through a diffusing lens to diffuse its light, which illuminates the object being photographed. The light from this beam, "disturbed" by the object, falls upon the photographic plate. These two beams intersect forming an interference pattern that is recorded on the photographic plate as a hologram. You can then shine a laser (pure beam of light), now a "reconstruction beam", through the hologram and get the whole image projected as a three dimensional object. You can even walk all the way around some projected images and see them from below and above as a real three dimensional object.[41] In the first Star Wars film, Princess Leah was projected as a hologram to warn and instruct Luke Skywalker.

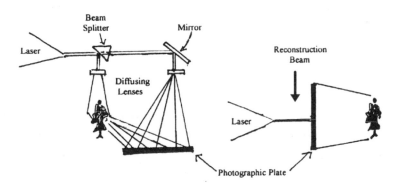

Figure 6.2: Procedure for Producing a Hologram

Memories, as holograms, make sense. When a stimulus (a situation, word, smell, etc.) triggers a memory by focusing a "laser beam" or "reconstruction beam" of attention on our stored hologram, a complete three dimensional memory with all its aspects is projected on our consciousness.[42] Frank Lake, a 1980's researcher studying trauma in utero, claims that memories from our developmental time in the womb act as holographic templates to orchestrate our perception of reality.[43]

Candace Pert sees the whole body as a chemical hologram, with information molecules being produced and binding to receptor sites on every cell. These information molecules (a variety of transmitters, peptides, hormones, factors and protein ligands) could be the triggers or "reconstruction beams" for anchoring information in the body as memory or retrieving memories that will determine our emotions and actions in accordance with the experiences of our life.[44]

The hippocampus of the brain, associated with producing memory, has receptor sites for virtually all the neuropeptides. Biochemical changes at the receptor sites appear to be molecularly involved in the development of memory. Ligards, small molecules that bind to cellular receptors and convey information messages to the cells, will change the membrane of the hippocampal cells to either take in neural information or not, affecting the choice of information we retain in memory.[45]

Emotions play an important part in determining how we filter our world, thus determining what information we will retain, and our take on reality. Repressed traumas caused by overwhelming emotions can be stored in a body part, thereafter affecting our ability to move or in some cases even feel that body part.[46]

"It makes no difference to the brain/body whether something actually happened or not. What we feel about an experience creates our "reality", our model of the world. Emotion releases hormonal patterns, which activate circulation, muscles and organic response as well as etching memory. Again, the brain and body respond in exactly the same way to both real and imagined experience".[47]

—*Gordon Stokes and Daniel Whiteside*

"There is always a biochemical potential for change and growth."[48] Focusing our attention, intention on coherence can assist us to restructure our memories and organize or reorganize the complex structures within our body.

Vibration Into Matter—the Life Force

"We delude ourselves with the thought that we know much more about matter than about a "metaphysical" mind or spirit and so we overestimate material causation and believe that it alone affords us a true explanation of life. But matter is just as inscrutable as mind." [49]

—Carl Jung

Plato, as well as many spiritual traditions, believed we existed before having a body. Rupert Sheldrake proposed the idea of a "morphogenic field", a vibrational template responsible for organizing vibrations into material systems.[50] For me, it is not such a leap of understanding to think of life as being stepped down from reciprocal space, into slower frequencies, as a reconstruction beam (intention) illuminates our vibrational hologram into material structure.

There are many mysteries about the occurrence and development of life. One that has mystified developmental biologists for decades is the mechanism of cellular differentiation that occurs at about eight days following conception in the developing embryo.[51,52] The fertilized egg (which in itself is a mystery) begins to divide into a hollow ball of cells called the blastocyst. Each cell has identical DNA, half from the mother and half from the father. Then suddenly following implantation into the uterine lining, the cells begin to migrate and differentiate. Some of the cells become Ectoderm making up our nervous system, skin and hair. Some become Mesoderm making up our muscles, blood vessels, and internal organs. The rest become Endoderm forming our gut and reproductive organs. Each cell perfectly migrates to its position, shutting off parts of the DNA sequence and only producing proteins that perfectly suit the cell they have been assigned.

DNA is the master code for our proteins and we thought it might instruct cell differentiation. But it has no mechanism for directing cells in such a mammoth migration. Perhaps the cell differentiation process exists as much in reciprocal space/time (as a morphic resonance) as in direct space/time.

In the 1940's Harold Burr, a neuroanatomist at Yale University, studied the shape of energy fields, the electro-magnetic fields generated by living plants and animals, using conventional voltmeters that supplied data at micro-voltage levels. He discovered, while studying the developing electrical axis in salamanders, (an electrical field aligning with the brain and spinal cord), that this axis originates in *unfertilized* salamander eggs, well before the egg is fertilized or differentiates. Also, the electromagnetic field around the developing embryonic salamander was roughly shaped like that of the adult animal instead of the fairly amorphous embryo. Burr also experimented with the electrical fields around developing seedlings, of many different plants.[53]

At the same time in Russia, Semyon Kirlian developed Kirlian photography (electrography) to study electrical fields in the body. His photographs showed the discharge patterns surrounding and produced from living objects in the presence of a high frequency, high voltage, and low amperage electrical field. These discharge patterns were captured on photographic film inserted between the object and the electrode. With this technology, Kirlian was able to translate Burr's work with seedlings into a visual electrical corona. Amazingly, the electrical field of the seedlings resembled the adult plant rather than the little two-leafed seedling. From these studies, Burr theorized there was a growth template, a map, generated by the organism's individual electromagnetic field.[54]

The electro-magnetic or bioenergetic field, lying around the physical body, with its higher vibrational frequency has been termed the etheric body.[55] Research suggests that within its energetic map, the etheric body carries spatial information on how the physical body of the developing embryo will grow, and guides repair following damage or disease in adult organisms.[56]

"The physical body is so energetically connected and dependent upon the etheric body for cellular guidance that the physical body cannot exist without the etheric body."[57]

— *Richard Gerber*

William Tiller proposes that Deltrons (intentions, thoughts or goals) connect reciprocal space— with direct space/time. Somehow the "would-be" human has the intention, life force, drive, to come into material existence, so matter is transduced out of reciprocal space into direct space/time, and life begins.[58]

"We are magnificant manifestations of the life force."
                    —*Virginia Satir* [59]

Ernst Runair Holland, neurophysiologist, states "Our intimate thoughts, dreams, desires are the result of electromagnetic field action on the brain and nervous system, which gives rise to matter." These thoughts, desires and dreams formulate vibrational patterns, which could in turn determine structure. You can't influence the energetic system without also influencing the structural system, and vice versa. [60]

Must not humans, and all life forms, be capable of utilizing the entire available information field of reciprocal space as the playground to come into being, bringing our dreams and intentions out of high energy patterns into the lower energy patterns of matter we recognize as life? In other words, everyone can write and rewrite their own book of life, through the remarkable drive and malleability of the human spirit. Through empirical science, it appears we can finally understand what the ancients have told us for millennia, that we all have equal opportunity to access whatever reality we choose. In choosing coherence, sound, music, play, creativity, and loving from the heart, the opportunity to affect the collective consciousness in an expanded way, becomes manifest.

CHAPTER SEVEN

Sound — the Cosmic Motor

"Few people fully appreciate the extent to which sounds in the environment influence and condition human behavior."
—*Barry Truax* [1]

I sit with all my instruments around me, now very aware of how each has brought coherence to my life and helped to structure my learning. My own voice resonates my inner being to the world in emotional outbursts, language, and song. The drum and rattles, sophisticated versions of the first pots, pans, and measuring spoons I beat on, mimic the familiar rhythm of my mother's heart beat. The piano is an elaborate version of my first xylophone that introduced me to varying pitches and an understanding of the elaborate harmonics, overtones, and patterns inherent in language. The violin with its rich wood vibration, energizes and releases the deepest emotions of my soul. The guitar allows me to blend my voice, rhythm, tones, patterns, and emotions with others.

The slower vibration of sound, compared to other vibrations like light, materializes as one of our first perceptual vibrations with hearing being one of our most important senses in utero and throughout life and our last sense to go at death. The influence of sound begins even before the rhythm of the mother's heartbeat establishes the first pattern for the embryonic brain to synchronize with. Embryos are thought to respond to sound as early as 23 days after conception and three month fetuses respond within five seconds to frequencies higher or lower than the range of the ear, prior to development of the cochlea and auditory nerve. This suggests skin and bone conduction.[2,3] It continues through the development of speech, from the early sounds of the mother's voice in utero, to the baby listening to and mimicking the sounds and finally to the elegance of self generated speech and song.

Sound has the capacity to energize us, make us more responsive to other sensory input; connect us to our society through music and rhythm; and assist us in understanding patterns in art, language, and mathematics. Sound helps to orchestrate our thought patterns and facilitates us sharing those thoughts through expressive language and music. Sound even effects the structural organization in the embryo.

Our Bodies As Cymatic Systems

"In the beginning was the word..."
—Bible

According to Parmahansananda Yogananda, a great yogic teacher, the sound Aum ("OM") is believed to be the cosmic vibration out of which all was manifest.[4] Astronomers discovered that sound vibrations coming from the Big Bang have orchestrated the patterns within galaxy clusters and the huge voids of space.[5] These sound vibrations orchestrated a specific 3D pattern with a nearly periodic spacing between galaxies of about 390 million light years.[6] As in the galaxies, sound vibrations may provide the patterns that form the structure of our cells, and ultimately our physical structure.

"As is well known, sound has great power over inorganic matter. By means of sound it is possible to cause geometric figures to form on sand and also to cause objects to be shattered. How much more powerful, then, must be the impact of this force on the vibrating, living substance of our sensitive bodies"?
—Roberto Assagiolio, Psychoanalyst

Cymatics, the study of tone on shape changes of both organic and inorganic matter, might explain how we first take shape as an embryo. Cymatics researchers, German physicist Ernst Chladni and later Dr. Hans Jenny, studied the influence of waveforms on matter by transforming sound vibrations into physical forms.[7] They put sand, liquids, powders, and metal filings on steel discs or drumheads and photographed the intricate designs that took shape when they played a specific note or tone on a violin.[8]

The powerful sound waves from the violin vibrated both the air and disc or drumhead. According to the pitch of the note, the drumhead or disc would vibrate in a pattern. High notes vibrated very rapidly while low notes vibrated slowly. In the cymatics experiments, sand grains on the drumhead or steel disc would collect in areas that were not vibrating, forming beautiful symmetrical patterns.[9]

Using Cymatics, Dr. Peter Guy Manners discovered that specific vibrations cause water droplets to change shape. With higher frequencies the droplet shape developed a more elaborate latticework pattern than with low frequencies. When he used five frequencies together, especially the higher frequencies, he was able to get a three-dimensional structure in malleable plastic that resembled the specific enfolding of embryonic structures. He was the first to suggest that sound vibration causes matter to take shape and orchestrates the structure of the cell. Even the beautiful patterns seen in spider webs, snowflakes, and flowers are believed to take their shape from the sound vibrations in nature.[10] Sanskrit is said to be a perfect language because the cymatic patterns formed by any specific sound are the same as those of the Sanskrit letters representing the sound.[11]

"As the sound, so the shape and form".[12,13]
—*Peter Guy Manners*

"Living tissues are extremely responsive to coherent energy. Sound patterns help to structure the physical system."[14]
—*Donald Ingber*

As Jim and I were singing in the car on our way to the Colorado raft trip where I would discover I was pregnant, Breeze was already feeling the vibrational patterns of our song in her watery environment through her developing skin and body.[15] Our song hung in a vibrational sea with the other sounds that were orchestrating her developing form.

The earth has the greatest effect of any force on our physiology, so it would make sense that the cells of our body align with it.

The earth's sound pattern, called the Schumann resonance, is a series of quick, rhythmic sound pulses that are measured in cycles per second or Hertz. This resonance has historically remained around 7.83 Hz, with some recent fluctuations as high as 9.0 Hz,[16] Not surprising, each of our cells and organs have a specific resonant frequency of 7.8 – 8 Hz also. Even the alpha brain wave patterns, which make it easier to learn, and the coherent heart vibrate at between 8-12 Hz.[17]

> *"All life within the envelope of Earth's vibratory influence attempts to "match" base frequencies to that of the Earth. To this end, each cell of your body is constantly shifting patterns of energy to achieve harmonic resonance to the reference signals of our planet."*[18]
> —*Gregg Braden*

All the chemical and electrical reactions and processes of our bodies follow patterns imposed by sound vibration from our environment. We, in the U.S. and Canada can easily match a B natural pitch because it's the pitch of our 60 Hz electrical system. In Europe, people easily match the G sharp pitch, which corresponds to their 50 Hz electricity.[19] Once my wonderful jazz musician husband forgot his electronic tuner, so he tuned up to the "B" of the vacuum as workers cleaned the conference hall for his performance.

Because we are so sensitive to vibrations, incoherent sound has the potential to create disharmony or dis-ease within our vibrational field. When I was pregnant with Breeze, ultrasound had just become popular for hearing the fetal heart beat. We often think of sound, especially if we can't hear it, as harmless, but Jim and I had concerns about the use of ultrasound on the delicate developing structures of our unborn child. In searching the literature, we found studies from Japan that showed a greater risk of problems in newborns after prenatal ultrasound, and Robert Mendelsohn, M.D., found that ultrasound might cause the destruction of DNA and delay normal maturation in the fetus.[20,21]

Sound and Energy

"Music is the electrical soil in which the spirit lives, thinks and invents."
— Beethoven

Dr. Tomatis asserts that the first function of the ear is to "charge" the brain and body with energy, which nourishes the functions of thought, reflection, and creativity.[22] After a music fest, or singing and jamming with friends, it takes several hours before I can go to sleep. In fact, I have stayed up whole nights playing music without needing to sleep, but I still felt energized. This charging occurs through the vestibular system.

As I look at Figure 7.1 (p. 94) of a 2-month-old embryo, two features immediately stand out: the perfectly formed semicircular canals, inner ear structures that are key parts of the vestibular system and the very large heart, elegant generator of our largest electromagnetic field. The vestibular system, fully developed by five months after conception, is the vestibule or entryway into the brain. The vestibular nuclei, a group of neurons lying in the medulla oblongata and pons of the brain stem, connect impulses coming from the semicircular canals to the Reticular Activating System (RAS). The RAS is a group of nerves which carry impulses to the neocortex, "waking it up" and increasing its excitability and responsiveness to incoming sensory stimuli from the environment.

By four to five months in utero, the 8th cranial nerve pair, carrying auditory information from the ear to the brain is the first sensory nerve pair to develop. The high frequency of the mother's voice, heard through the amniotic fluid, is believed to energetically charge the brain of the fetus via the vestibular/RAS system.[23] The semicircular canals and the cochlea share a common chamber, fluid, and the 8th cranial nerve. Thus, hearing is influenced by information passing through the vestibular system, and the vestibular system is influenced by sound.[24]

Higher sound frequencies, with their faster vibration and higher energy (as seen in cymatics), cause more intricate patterns to arise in the brain. We instinctively talk to babies with a higher voice, called "Parentese", which we now know energizes the baby's brain,

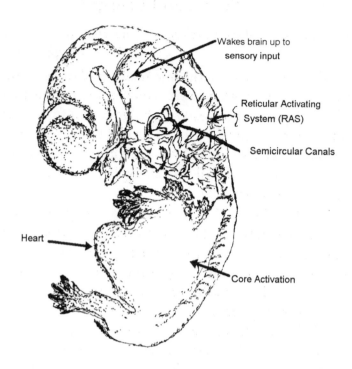

Wakes brain up to
sensory input

Reticular Activating
System (RAS)

Semicircular Canals

Heart

Core Activation

Figure 7.1: Vestibular System of Two Month Old Embryo

making it more alert to all sensory input and able to take in specific patterns and rhythms, thus aiding learning.[25]

The upper range of sound is so important to the energy of the body, that factory workers, who have had their upper range of hearing damaged from constant high frequency machinery sounds, exhibit depression, low muscle tone, and lower energy states. This same kind of damage to the delicate hearing apparatus can occur prior to birth and can affect or even kill the developing child. Mothers that live near jet airports or have exposure to loud sounds of long duration during pregnancy are more likely to have stillborn or low birth weight babies, with a higher incidence of autism.[26,27,28]

Sound and Balance

"Everything passes through the opening of the ear; we speak, read, sing and dance with our ears, we maintain a vertical posture, establish relational dynamics and laterality thanks to our ears".
                                            —A. A. Tomatis

By five to six months in utero, the fetus can actually process sound, which stimulates muscle tone (especially of the core muscles), equilibrium, and flexibility.[29] These core muscles control posture and maintain balance throughout life.[30,31] It is easy to ascertain how energetic and open to learning a person is by just looking at his/her posture. Dr. Tomatis in working with many depressed people noticed that their postures immediately communicated their state of depression; they slumped, dragged, and had a hard time standing up straight.

The newborn hears and moves in rhythm to the mother's voice in the first minutes of life. There are no random movements; every movement of the newborn has meaning, with particular movements being linked to particular sounds.[32] For example, with a sudden loud sound the baby will throw out its arms and legs in a Moro Reflex.[33] In response to his mother's voice, he will turn toward her. Studies done using high-speed film show that newborns and infants have a complete and individual repertoire of body movements that precisely synchronize with syllables or sub-syllables of a speaker's voice.[34] This important matching of movement to words, or "entrainment", starts in utero at about 4 ½ months and leads to full development of the vestibular system and the ability to language successfully.[35,36]

Jeffrey taught me much as we worked on his speech and reading difficulties. He was labeled dyslexic and hyperactive. He couldn't sit up straight, "noodling" in his seat, he missed what was being said to him, and constantly spoke in monosyllables. During recess he could run forever, but if someone ran in front of him, or he had to make a quick turn, he would lose his balance. He had to hold onto a chair for balance if I asked him to do standing cross-crawls slowly.

Tomatis believes balance is the second function of the ear in that movement and "equilibrium" are linked to the vestibular part of the ear, providing the ability to stand up vertically. He states that establishment of that verticality with balance is essential to language development.[37] Doing regular balance and vestibular activities with Jeffrey, mainly Brain Gym®, produced a very different person. Just taking slow, balanced walks, he would suddenly begin talking in full sentences. He became calm and focused, his language became complex and appropriate and finally he could read.

"We acquire the ability to understand (comprehend) sounds only as we integrate vestibular sensations. The vestibular system influences motor control and motor planning necessary to use the fine muscles to produce intelligible speech. A child may not talk very much or well until they move around. When a child begins to swing or run, they may suddenly talk, sing or shout. Speech and language skills improve along with balance, movement and motor planning skills."[38]

— *Sally Goddard*

Rhythm and Steady Beat

An audiotape of in utero sounds made by Alfred Tomatis propelled me deeply into the world of the fetus. I had an experience of the fetus floating in surround sound, right next to the stomach, digestive tract, heart, and lungs. The dripping, churning sounds of digestion are fairly innocuous, but stomach rumblings can peak at 85–95 decibels. Normal human speech lies at only 60 decibels.[39] The fetus, far from being inert in this noisy incubator, is very active and responsive to all kinds of stimuli from inside and outside[40].

For me, the most noticeable sound was the mother's rhythmic breathing, which sounded just like the ocean waves lapping gently on a Hawaiian beach. It's easy to understand why people place their towels right next to perfect strangers on a beach and don't feel their space has been invaded. They are back in the womb, secure with the rhythm of the surf, a remembrance of the soothing breathing sounds in utero.

The other controlling sounds in utero are the loud beat of the heart, and the rhythmic flow of blood through the mother's blood vessels. Heartbeat is such a strong pattern that a human fetus will respond rhythmically to a tympanist during an orchestral performance within 25 weeks after conception.[41]

Heartbeat is a touchstone pattern for the developing embryo whose heart beats well before it has blood to pump, at 41 days after conception.[42] The mother's heart rhythm, either coherent or incoherent, allows the embryo and fetus to discern whether the mother is safe or in danger. If the mother's heart rhythm is coherent, it forms the framework for our ability to maintain a steady beat pattern throughout our lives.

The embryo and fetus are constantly moving with the mother's heartbeat and body movement. Steady beat continues after birth with rhythmic movement as a baby rides on the mother's body or is rocked in a caretaker's arms. Our human affinity for steady beat is innately demonstrated by the rhythmic rocking we fall into when someone hands us a baby.

Mothers instinctively nurse their babies on the left first, with the baby's right ear against the mother's heart, which will allow it to assess the safety or danger of the environment from the mother's coherent or incoherent heart pattern. The left ear is available to pick up the tone, melody, and emotional quality of the mother's voice and environment.[43]

Steady beat is basic to our love for the beat within music—where the bass carries the rhythm that moves our body during a dance or annoys us at night as a teenager turns up the volume and cruises through our neighborhood doing his courting ritual. It helps us organize our breathing, walking, dancing patterns and assists us to make patterns of our incoming sensory information in order to learn easily.[44]

In Savanga, Alaska, a small village just 35 miles from Russia, all the Eskimo music stems from the heart rhythm. This appears to be true throughout the world. Ancient instruments like the frame drum depicted on a wall painting in Catal Huyuk in Turkey from at least 8,000 years ago was undoubtedly built to mimic the heartbeat, as are drums today.[45] In checking preferred drum rhythms worldwide, the one most frequently preferred is the coherent beat of the human heart. In horror movies, film producers use the heartbeat rhythm to subliminally capture people's attention and then speed it up and make it incoherent during dramatic scenes to activate fear in the audience.

During maternal stress when coherent steady beat is missing, the fetal heart rate and breathing also becomes incoherent. If maternal stress is chronic, this could be a possible cause of SIDS (sudden infant death syndrome) in newborns. Babies with irregular (incoherent) heartbeats face a 41 fold greater risk of SIDS in their first year than babies with a regular heartbeat.[46] Incoherent heartbeats and breathing can be seen in monkeys or orphaned children who have been isolated from their mothers right after birth and left without movement and touch. They rock back and forth in an attempt to somehow reestablish the steady beat movement they missed.[47] Therapists now realize this self-stimulation is an attempt to tap into a coherent pattern that will facilitate their brain growth and learning process.

When parents and caregivers rock infants and toddlers and pat or burp them in steady beat, the child's ability to sense and use beat begins. Simple rhymes like "Patty Cake, Patty Cake" are great to instill steady beat in the child. Take the baby's hands and slowly and gently clap them together during each phrase—clap during "patty cake" then clap again during the next "patty cake", and then during "baker's" and next "man", etc. Do not clap on each syllable (pa – ti – cake) as it will fracture the rhythm and set up incoherence in the brain.[48]

Nursery rhymes and children's songs are elegant ways to establish steady beat competency early. The child can rock or pat her knees (and other body parts) while listening to the rhythms and songs, and "chime in" with the words and/or melody when it becomes familiar.[49]

Steady beat underlies our ability to pick up the pattern of language, express that pattern as verbal language, and translate that pattern to symbols to read the language. Many of today's youth and more than 50% of adults in the U.S. are deficient in steady beat competency and, thus, are missing the foundation patterns for learning and languaging well. Phyllis Weikart, in testing large samples of high school students, found the following:

Percent of students exhibiting steady beat competency:

Year	% of Females	% of Males
1981	80 – 85%	60 – 66 %
1991	48%	30%

From the figures, it is not surprising there are 6 boys for every girl in special education programs, which focus on reading difficulties. In 1998, when testing in elementary schools, Dr. Weikart found that less than 10% of students had steady beat competency, which should be in place by 2-3 years of age for adequate linguistic development.[50]

According to Dr. Weikart, English is the only un-metered language, being a collection of sounds from different languages, making it all the more important to ground English with steady beat.

Touch, tapping out the beat on a child's back or hands, and movement, as when the child marches or claps their own hands, are the strongest anchors to provide a memory of the pattern. Then add a word or phrase, and using natural speech, have the child mimic you. Once steady beat is an innate part of our body rhythm, we can advance to rhythm changes in music and language easily.

The patterns in Mozart's music are excellent for steady beat patterning and, therefore, have been found to assist learning. College students who heard 10 minutes of Mozart's *Sonata for Two Pianos in D major (K.448)* raised their IQ scores on tests of spatial-temporal reasoning, a skill related to math.[51,52] Other researchers have used this same sonata to improve the spatial-temporal reasoning of an Alzheimer's patient and to reduce the number of seizures in epileptics. A new study shows that sustained, complex rhythms have an even greater impact than Mozart's sonata, as much as 20% more, on spatial-temporal reasoning skills.[53] Music that elicits a coherent heart rate variability pattern, whether complex or not, also assists in decreasing heart rate, blood pressure, and the amount of lactic acid in muscles during exercise or physical exertion, thus reducing muscle tension and increasing efficiency.[54]

What we hear in utero, especially the heart pattern, affects our hearing for the rest of our lives, either enhancing it or limiting it. The Chinese recognized this heart and hearing connection when they said: "The color of the Southern direction is red, it is related to the Heart which opens into the ears..."[55] Asians seem to be much more attuned to the importance of sound in utero and even have a practice, called Tae-gyo. In Tae-gyo they begin the education of the baby by exposing expectant mothers to music that relaxes the embryo and fetus and has a pattern that assists learning development.[56] Babies come into the world already connected through sound.

The Sound of Music

"As neither the enjoyment nor the capacity of producing musical notes are faculties of the least direct use to man in reference to his ordinary habits in life, they must be ranked amongst the most mysterious with which he is endowed."
—*Charles Darwin (1871)*

"All human beings... and only human beings... have language and music. They are hallmarks of what it means to be a human being."
—*Donald A. Hodges[57]*

Breeze started her out-of-womb life with a song. In the low light of the delivery room, just moments into the world and still attached to me via the placenta, Jim held her and sang to her. She listened to his tonal rainbow, full of his love and delight with her.

As with all babies, Breeze was born with the ability to perceive and process basic musical sounds and patterns.[58] For fun Jim and I sang often to her, the lullabies of our youth, rowdy college songs, and our favorite folk songs and in an attempt to get her to sleep, or to ease the wailing of teething bouts. Our singing consisted of musical patterns with rising and falling pitches called musical contours that 8-9 month old infants respond to, even if the same pattern is repeated in another key. The responses of infants to musical contour are the same as adults, showing that brain specialization for contour is present at a very early age.[59]

It is believed by researchers that infants are born with the ability and longing to compose music. By the age of nine, children can produce original compositions naturally, using the same processes as professional composers. This ability ties directly into a child's understanding of pattern within sounds and their innate creative processes. When children can retain sound patterns because of the coherence in their lives, it facilitates their ability to compose music and also to understand and create usable patterns in all areas of learning.[60,61,62]

According to Robert Jordain, of all the animals on our planet, the human brain has discovered music—the ability to manipulate patterns of sound far more complex than any other animal's brain can manage. Our brains encode relationships between melody, passages, chords, and rhythms for the sensations of sound to arise. "We model patterns upon patterns upon patterns, right up to the movement of a symphony."[63]

The power of music to assist the brain in understanding patterns can be seen on SATs (Scholastic Achievement Tests) scores for verbal and math skills. Students with music in their school curriculum scored far higher on standardized tests than students with no music in the curriculum. High school students scored an average of 35 points higher on the verbal and math sections if music education, music appreciation or music instruction was involved in their overall education.

Students with four or more years of music education scored dramatically higher on SATs than those that had no music.[64] Music in the curriculum was also found to assist social interactions and self-esteem. Students with music worked better in groups and got along more with both peers and superiors alike. Their overall self-esteem was higher, and their chance of dropping out of school was much less. Of great interest to me was the research showing improvement of four grade levels of reading in "low readers" after just 6 months of instrumental music instruction.[65]

At an English cathedral, and also at Cambridge, the Master of Choristers found the reading age of all their choirboys improved by 12 months within 6 months of their joining the choir. Listening, vocalizing, learning to hear pitch and rhythm, as well as reading the written music, enhanced all their learning skills.[66] Harmonic toning, as in singing or chanting, activates the whole cranium and

Music and SAT Scores

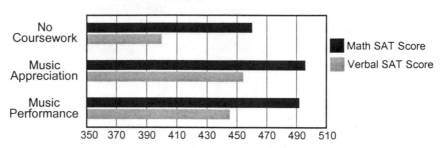

Long-Term Music Study & SAT Scores

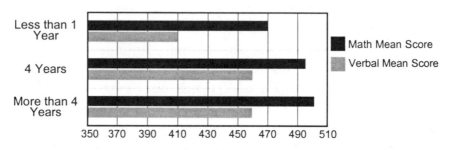

Figure 7.2: Music and SAT Scores on Verbal and Mathematical Testing

increases respiratory rate, and flow of cerebral spinal fluid in the brain, thus optimizing brain function.[67]

Musical training beginning at an early age has an abundance of rewards. In brain studies of musicians versus non-musicians, music was shown to greatly assist fine motor development and significantly increase gray matter volume in both the left and right sensorimotor cortexes and the left basal ganglion that orchestrates movement. The research also showed a significantly higher EEG coherence, a more receptive and 25% larger auditory cortex, and greater cerebellum and corpus callosum differentiation. [68,69,70,71]

I am impressed with organizations like Kindermusik, Musikgarten, Music Together, Music with Mar and many more whose programs are excellent for integrating all the elements of sound, movement, touch, and music in the pre-school years of life. These programs begin with whole families exploring sound when the children are very young. They incorporate sound with real instruments and singing to energize and alert the body and mind. Families participate in integrative, cross-lateral movements and steady beat to assist the process of pattern finding in their children. The child get lots of touch through play and massage and develops a lifelong love of music and rhythm, which makes pattern seeing and learning infinitely easier.[72]

I experienced first hand the complex benefit of music for learning while playing cymbals in a community 4th of July parade band. Our group was comprised of students, ages 9 to 21 years of age and some of their music teachers. Incredibly, not only did they follow a bandleader, play complex instruments, read complex musical scores and make beautiful music together, they marched in time and precise physical formation with all the other band members. It was awesome!!! Every part of the mind/body system was engaged.

Cecily, a neighbor, teaches in an inner city middle school where children face many challenges in their homes and also with learning. Knowing the importance of real sound for brain and learning development, Cecily was able to procure enough violins for each of her students to use during the school year. The violin with its high frequency vibrations stimulates the whole mind/body system. Over the year the students became an impressive group of violinists as well as good students with positive energy and self-confidence.

Single reed instruments such as the clarinet, saxophone, or recorder also vibrate and energize the body as the mouthpiece rests against the upper teeth sympathetically vibrating all the bones in the head. So, even in an orchestra or concert band where clarinets traditionally sit right in front of trombones and trumpets, making it difficult for them to hear what they are playing, they can actually feel the sound through their teeth and head.[73]

Music must be an integral part of every curriculum in the schools, with children singing many times during the day, if only to sing their assignment back to the teacher. Learning to "play" a musical instrument, first by exploring rhythm and tone for the fun of it before introducing music, must occur at least weekly in the classroom. Music must continue in the curriculum, as it does in most European schools and all Asian schools, until the child/young adult graduates. Besides energizing their whole system, keeping the brain focused and attentive to the cognitive patterns we are attempting to teach in language and math, music allows for greater sensitivity to the vast vibrational fields that enrich life and make the whole planet more coherent and pleasurable.

Hearing and Listening

"The yearning to be listened to and understood is a yearning to escape our separateness and bridge the space that divides us. We reach out and try to overcome that separateness by revealing what's on our minds and in our hearts, hoping for understanding."
—*Michael Nichols*[74]

According to Tomatis, the third function of the ear is hearing and by extension, "listening". Listening involves the whole body.[75] The following symbol from the Chinese word for *"to listen"* involves not just the ear, but also the heart, eyes, and the rest of the body in undivided attention. The literal translation is: "Use the heart to listen and both the messages from the outside world as well as from within will come straight into the heart." It is a profound expression of the manifestation of life force through sound.

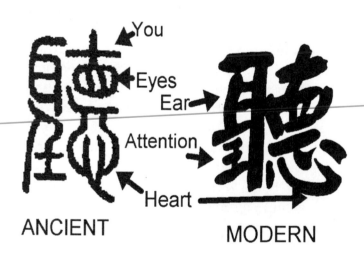

You
Eyes
Ear
Attention
Heart
ANCIENT   MODERN

Figure 7.3: Chinese Symbol—TO LISTEN

My mother, through her example, taught me to always listen and keep the communication lines open. Perhaps it's the most "right thing" I did with Breeze, even though it was almost impossible at times not to jump in with judgments or solutions. Breeze told me everything, many things I didn't want to know. I learned to bite my tongue when she told me of her explorations with drugs, boys, tattoos, etc., because if I could listen to the end, I was always struck by her discoveries and the wise choices she made in support of her highest good. We all have to explore our current worlds, and make our own mistakes, often to the fear of our loved ones.

I hear kids today saying "Don't dis me". Dis indicates negation, lack, invalidation, deprivation. These developing humans are desperately asking us not to dis-miss, dis-card, dis-able, dis-regard them. In other words, "Don't disconnect from me, I want to be listened to". The least we can do as parents and loved ones, is to listen.

How Do I Listen?
"How Do I Listen to others?
As if everyone were my Master speaking to me
His Cherished Last Words."
—Hafiz[76]

CHAPTER EIGHT

Language — Sound In Motion

*"Both music and language are about long,
highly organized streams of sound".*
—Robert Jourdain[1]

Sound is the grossest of subtle energies, stretching across a huge spectrum from 15 to well over 20,000 cycles/second (HZ). Below 15 Hz is infra-sound, and above 20,000Hz is ultrasound, both we experience in our bodies though we can't actually hear them with our ears. Human speech lies between 125 Hz and 8,000Hz.[2] With each sound there is a fundamental sound, above which are the harmonics and overtones that give us the full analog (range, depth and color) of sound. If you have had the joy of listening to chanting in a cathedral, you know what that analog of sound feels like in your body with all the tones and overtones melting into one another, vibrating your bones and filling every cell with sound.

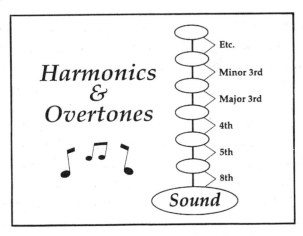

Figure 8.1: Fundamental sounds and overtones/harmonics

In the following sonogram of British and American spoken phrases, the upper levels of vibration, above 20,000 Hz., are above the range of hearing but are felt within the bones and skin and affect our understanding of language.

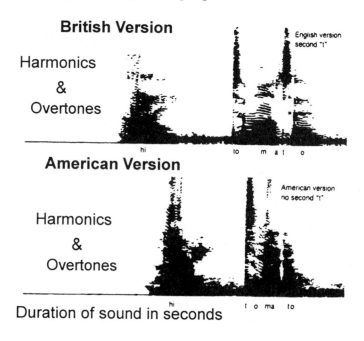

Figure 8.2: Sonogram of British and American Spoken Words[3]

In order for children to learn language, they must have the full spectrum of the language, even the harmonics and overtones that lie above the range of hearing. CD's, most audiotapes, computer-generated sound, TV, and many instruments today are electronic and digitized. Digitizing takes out any overtones or harmonics above 20kHz, which is above the direct range of hearing, causing many of the beneficial high frequency sounds to be lost. We have also lost those rich high frequencies in our homes with low soundproof ceilings, carpeting and cushioned furniture.[4] Many musicians prefer listening to the old vinyl records, because they still present sound as a full analog.

I believe it is fine to play tapes and CD's like Mozart to children because of the strong, coherent pattern. It helps the child to entrain with and understand the pattern and hopefully translate that ability to other pattern finding tasks. But I strongly feel that stories read on a tape or CD or listening to TV can be harmful because these lack the full spectrum of harmonics and overtones so essential in learning language. Using real instruments and the human voice is optimal, because they energize us and provide the full spectrum of sound.

Our bodies are living bio-oscillators, and vibrating them with our own voice or real musical instruments should be an integral part of our daily life.[5] Children need to be hearing the language, as parents talk to them in ever increasingly complex sentences while they mature. And the child then needs to speak in response, mimicking and matching sounds and speech in order to understand it. In homes where there is a lot of parent-child communication, language development is much faster, with children using 131 words at 20 months and 295 words at 24 months.[6] A recent study compared the number of words in the vocabulary of an average 14-year-old in 1950 and 1999. The results are very telling:

1950	25,000 words
1999	10,000 words[7]

Young children, still so tuned into vibrations, love to play with the language, saying words over and over to feel them in their mouth, to vibrate them throughout their bodies, and to get other people's attention with them.

Many (maybe most) teenagers today have a distinct "sitcom language", consisting of monosyllables and incomplete sentences. Typical phrases are: "It's like", "you know", "sort of", "don't go there" etc. Jane Healy points out that the way we speak is a reflection of the way we think.[8] Many Americans even watch TV during meals, which inhibits family discussion, so necessary for language development and human connection. As I was growing up, no matter what, the whole family sat down to dinner together and discussed everything, from school to summer plans. As an open forum, it wasn't always calm and rational, but it did keep us connected as a family and allowed us to speak our thoughts and emotions.

Don Campbell compares sounding our own voice to massaging and vibrating our bodies from the inside out,[9] and David White, an Irish poet, calls speech "astonishing intimacy". The most intimate thing we can do, he says, is to amplify the vibration of our thoughts into an audible vibration in our vocal cords and resonant mouth chamber. And then send this vibration out across the air waves to vibrate the tympanic membrane, inner ear, and finally the whole body and spirit of another person.[10]

The Sound of Dyslexia

"Everything happens as if human behavior were largely conditioned by the manner in which one hears."
—*Guy Berard, M.D.*[11]

Hearing is harder than vision, which deals with objects which are both definite and possess duration. Sounds that reach our ears are fleeting, fluctuating, and constantly changing, yet essential to learning. If a child can't hear the language, she can't mimic it to speak properly, and she can't understand the visual symbols to sound it out in order to read. Because of their inability to pick up the patterns that sound provides, deaf students I taught at the Community College of Denver tended to have a more difficult time with cognitive learning than did blind students.

How does this lack of sound patterning tie into the label of dyslexia, which for so long was considered a seeing problem? Many researchers now believe that dyslexia begins in utero with maternal stress that affects the semicircular canals. The resulting underdeveloped vestibular system affects the ability to hear.

Sound helps determine vestibular development, and the developing vestibular system assists the body to hear sound.[12] When a pregnant woman is in a state of coherence, moving, talking, and singing, the embryo and fetus are using the sound coming through the amniotic fluid to develop their vestibular system. As the developing fetus moves in rhythm to incoming sounds, input from the vestibular system "primes" the entire nervous system to grow and function effectively.[13] These specific developmental steps must occur in utero to assure a solid framework later on for integrative hearing, interpreting the expressions of others, verbalizing, artistic and written expression, and finally reading. If these steps are disrupted or delayed, children can end up with behavioral patterns that we label as Dyslexia, ADHD, Learning Disabled and even Emotionally Handicapped.[14]

Dyslexia appears to start, as does everything in our life, with the perception of safety or lack of safety in the environment. With chronic stress before and after birth, the stress hormones cause the Moro and withdrawal reflexes to linger, which disrupts the normal development of other reflexes important for vestibular development and thus hearing. The consequences are a lack of balance, an immature central nervous system, hearing difficulties, poor sequencing and organizational skills, and hyperactivity.[15,16]

The Leading Ear

Perfectly developed at birth, the ear leads all the movement and reflex development, determining how the body moves. As the infant is allowed lots of movement and exploration, the reflexes that further grow the vestibular system develop, assisting hearing as well as visual development. As the baby then creeps and crawls, these earlier reflexes like the Moro reflex are naturally inhibited as the vestibular, visual, and proprioceptive (sense of muscle orientation in space) systems start to operate together for the first time.

Breeze appeared to me as both a miracle and nuisance at this developmental stage, as she explored her world on all fours. Nothing was safe from her wandering body, hands, and eyes as her now more coordinated movements gave her a sense of balance, space and depth, and synchronized feeling, seeing, and moving. This whole process provided the raw materials for perfect hearing and visual maturity, which naturally occurs at about 8 months given normal vestibular development.[17]

"As we move and interact with gravity, sensory receptors in the ear are activated, and impulses apprising the central nervous system about the position of the head in space are directed to various parts of the brain and down the spinal cord. It is believed that sensory impulses from the eyes, ears, muscles and joints must be matched to the vestibu-

lar input before such information can be reprocessed efficiently. If that is true, what we see, hear and feel makes sense only if the vestibular system is functioning adequately."

—Pyfer, J. & Johnson, R. 1981[18]

If the parents or caregivers do not allow the baby enough floor time on her belly to explore movement naturally, and/or attempt to help her performance so she can walk earlier, she never goes through the complex steps necessary to fully develop the vestibular system. Without these steps, aberrant reflexes may impair the vestibular system's ability to process and relay sound messages received by the ear to the language-processing center in the cortex. Therefore, the child develops sound discrimination problems and auditory/speech delays.[19]

Compounding the problem, stress lowers the immune system, making the baby more susceptible to all sorts of illnesses, including middle ear infections, asthma, allergies, and epileptic seizures. Middle ear infection appears to be the most wide spread early disease, affecting 2/3 of the children in the U.S. by two years of age. It is the most common cause of acquired hearing loss in children.[20, 21] The Levinson study shows that between 94 – 98% of children with dyslexia and learning disabilities had middle ear infections, allergies, or trauma.[22,23] Hearing and balance problems arise from these early infections, especially if the child is not physically active enough to grow the necessary nerve networks in the vestibular system.

Another factor that plays into a child being labeled with dyslexia has to do with which ear she relies on when hearing the language. The left hemisphere of the brain receives sounds more directly from the right ear, and the right hemisphere more directly from the left ear. The left hemisphere contains Wernekes and Broca's area for verbal language processing. As an infant begins to learn language, she will naturally use the right ear, which is sensitive to intensity, frequency, timbre, rhythm, the flow of sentences, and ordering. Because the right ear is more directly connected to the speech areas (Wernekes and Broca's), there is quicker communication between the voice and the brain. However, when infants are stressed, they will tend to use the left ear, whose auditory nerve goes into the right hemisphere and provides three-dimensional sound (which aids in hearing where the danger is located).

Under stress, if a child is attempting to hear and learn language, she will revert to using her left ear because survival is primary. Hence, the sounds of the language must go first to the right hemisphere (to assess where the danger lies) and then to the left for discriminating the words. The resulting delay in verbal comprehension may be between 4 – 6 milliseconds. This delay makes it difficult for the child to follow a list of verbal instructions, as she is still decoding the first two instructions when the third is being given, again resulting in dyslexic behavior.[24],[25],[26]

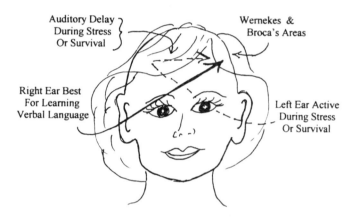

Figure 8.3: Ear/Hemisphere diagram showing auditory delay route

Many children can't discriminate tonal frequencies, missing part of the sound spectrum, which causes them to miss where a sentence begins and ends.[27] Others experience auditory distortion, missing the consonants and whistling sounds because they are covered by a vowel sound, or missing vowels because they are covered by the consonants. Some words are "heard" wrong, others slowly sorted, so the child has a hard time answering when she didn't hear the question as it was asked. She can't use her whole intellectual potential because of the strain and fatigue of trying to grasp the language.[28],[29]

From my travels and contact with foreign language speakers, I have a basic understanding of the difficulties these children must experience. Attempting to understand and use a foreign language can be stressful, especially if you want to be respected and get your basic needs met. In learning English, our children are attempting to do just that, get needs met and be respected. When I first hear a language, I have little clue as to where a word begins or ends, and in many cases, what letters are in use—as with Chinese, Russian or Polish. I took French in school, but attempting to follow it makes me extremely tired. I become very dependent on the tone qualities of speech and body language to somehow understand what is being said.

When we haven't heard the language enough to be able to speak it in a coherent way, it will be very hard to understand the symbols that represent the words and phrases of language to read it. I gained a perception of this by attempting to read Hebrew symbology. I think this is what our children experience when they are asked to read before they are fully competent in the spoken language. When the sounds of the symbols are presented and heard correctly, if a person can speak the language, they can use the symbols to read it.

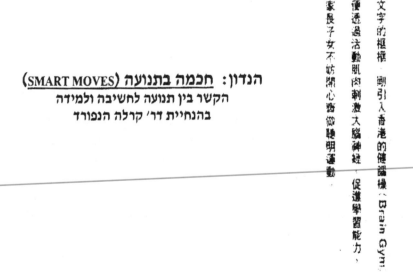

Figure 8.4: Hebrew and Chinese Symbolic Language Examples

Too Loud!!!

Another cause of dyslexic symptoms is hearing damage. As part of our sensory addiction, sound has become louder and louder, damaging the delicate structures of the inner ear and profoundly affecting our hearing. Exposure to loud sounds is the cause of hearing loss in over 28 million people in the U.S. today. Six percent of fourth graders, nine percent of ninth graders, and sixty-one percent of college freshmen have measurable hearing loss. Due to the noise in our environment, an average 25-year-old in the U.S. hears less well than the average 60-year-old in traditional African society.[30] In good classrooms, children only recognize 70% of one-syllable words, in poor classrooms, less than 30%. Distance from the speaker is also important with 89% correct comprehension at 6 feet, 55% at 12 feet, and only 36% at 24 feet.[31]

Any damage to the hearing mechanism will result in inaccurate imitation of the sound and difficulties with language. Hearing loss in the range of 500 Hz. results in poor perception of the voiceless consonants (m, n or p, t & f). This prevents children from learning easily and may be another source of confusion that fosters dyslexia.[32]

Hearing loss between 500 – 1000 Hz makes it impossible for a true appreciation of music; between 1000 – 2000 Hz hearing loss prevents one from singing in tune; and above 2000 Hz prevents hearing harmonics and other tonal qualities that make the voice pleasant and melodic.[33]

Steps to Dyslexia

The following are some of the steps that researchers are finding lead to the behavioral label of dyslexia.

1. Maternal stress elevates adrenalin and cortisol in the mother and developing embryo and fetus.
2. Stress sustains the withdrawal and Moro reflexes beyond the time they should be inhibited, thus delaying development of the reflexes necessary for normal vestibular system development.

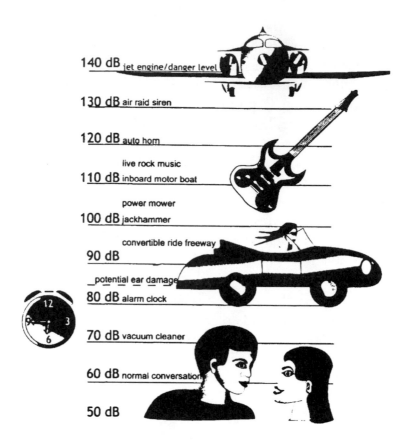

140 dB jet engine/danger level

130 dB air raid siren

120 dB auto horn

live rock music
110 dB inboard motor boat

power mower
100 dB jackhammer

convertible ride freeway
90 dB

potential ear damage
80 dB alarm clock

70 dB vacuum cleaner

60 dB normal conversation

50 dB

*Figure 8.5: Decibel (dB) readings
showing potential hearing damage*

3. Not enough exploratory movement or interactive language, leads to underdeveloped vestibular system and hearing.

4. An underdeveloped vestibular system leads to unstable balance, undeveloped head-righting reflexes, poor spatial awareness and orientation, hearing difficulties, and lack of eye teaming.

5. A reduced immune system makes the baby susceptible to middle ear infections, asthma, allergies, epileptic seizures and winter diseases like influenza. Boys born from May, June to July to mothers that had winter diseases, display more than twice the risk of developing dyslexia than boys

born in other months, accounting for 40% of all instances of dyslexia.[34]

6. Parents try to help the child's performance which over stimulates the child beyond its developmental level, causing dys-coordination and hearing difficulties the child tries to overcome by developing compensations.

7. Compensations lead to structural problems seen mostly in the eyes, backs, rigid muscles, and a homolaterality making it difficult for all the muscles of the body to work together.

8. Stress inhibits normal development of the right ear to left hemisphere preference for hearing and decoding language. Hearing delays of 0.4 – 0.9 millisecond make it difficult to hear the fast sounds of language.[35]

9. The child has a hard time discriminating sounds, words, or sentences and categorizing sounds or occluding miscellaneous sounds.

10. Fatigue occurs due to the futile attempts to follow the language. Hearing, speech and reading difficulties occur.

11. IF YOU CAN'T HEAR IT, IT'S DIFFICULT TO SPEAK IT OR SOUND OUT THE SYMBOLOGY TO READ IT. Dyslexia is twice as prevalent in the U.S. where the task of matching English sounds that make up a word to the symbols that represent it are dramatically at odds.[36]

12. This vulnerable situation can lead to behavioral problems including social withdrawal, ADHD, dyslexia, and emotional handicaps.[37,38,39,40,41]

Some of the top research dealing with dyslexia and how to eliminate it comes from Denmark. Rather than pushing reading remediation, as we tend to do in the U.S., the Danes immediately begin to work on the vestibular system, getting the child swinging, twirling, rolling, and using slow cross-lateral movements for balance. They also focus on singing, speaking, and improving the child's listening skills by putting them in a choir or other musical experience. Singing in a choir allows the child to hear himself in vibrational reference to others, learn to read by reading music, and gain the full range of sound necessary to understand the pieces of language. Reading is the culminating activity of their work, rather than the only therapy. Thus, by the time students graduate from school, there is 100% literacy in two languages, and their society isn't left with dyslexic adults.[42]

> *"Sound is vibration, motion and energy. If we hear no sound we perceive danger, for the totally silent world is a dead world. Sound passes through all levels of the brain, affecting not just the ear and the vestibular system, but also our bodies through bone conduction. The significance of sound for learning is immeasurable."*[43]
>
> —Sally Goddard

Sound, with all its vibrant colors for our life, may be one of our greatest gifts. In so many ways it connects us with others and our world, giving us the tools to express all that we are and all that we wish to become. Let us make music, sing, talk intimately, laugh, and enjoy the instrument we are, exchanging our vibrational waves with each other.

CHAPTER NINE

Play, Opener of the Heart

"A child's world is fresh and new and beautiful, full of wonder and excitement. It is our misfortune that for most of us that clear-eyed vision, that true instinct for what is beautiful and awe-inspiring, is dimmed and even lost before we reach adulthood."
—Rachel Carson

The Essence of Play

Growing up under the heavy yoke of the Puritan ethic, I reveled in every delicious moment of play, either alone or in joyous rough and tumble play with the wild assortment of neighborhood kids I grew up with.

My Aunts and Uncles farms in Iowa became favorite summer playgrounds, rich with cousins, haymows, and baby animals. I jumped, rolled, and climbed my way through the hot Iowa summers, my curiosity aflame like the fireflies that studded the sultry nights. Play included my family's love of camping in the mountains, complete with the stream and deep, enchanted forests I would explore for hours, my imagination fully engaged.

All these growing up play experiences taught me curiosity, how to create my dreams, and how to be in integrity with nature and other people. They shaped my love for life and the way I continue to see and explore my world as an adult.

When I speak of play, my meaning is that of sensuous, spontaneous, connected, explorative, safe, non-competitive, lost-in-the-moment, balanced, rough and tumble, joyful play that creates a mood of bliss, FLOW, and a sense of no time. Play, for me is the way the spirit authentically expresses itself.

According to Stuart L. Brown, MD and psychiatrist, play is: *"a spontaneous, non-stereotyped, intrinsically pleasurable activity, free of anxiety or other overpowering emotion, without a visible, clear-cut goal other than its own activity."*[1] Johan Herizinga, in his book *Homo Ludens (Man at Play)* stipulates that real play is in fact freedom, without compulsion or constraint, with the spur-of-the moment spontaneity that most of us adults remember from childhood.[2]

During college I spent two semesters in animal behavior and double that in psychology courses. Each behavior in humans and other animals appeared to have a specific function with survival of the species heading the list. Play behavior was never mentioned. Play has baffled biologists and psychologists because it appears to be frivolous with no apparent survival value.

Stuart L. Brown presented an example of this frivolous behavior at a Touch the Future Conference in early 1999. He had taken pictures for *National Geographic* of musk ox standing in a circle. This was not unusual, as musk ox often circle up with horns out to protect themselves and their offspring from predators. However, this time the musk ox were head in, gossip circle fashion, exposing their rears in a most vulnerable way. Suddenly one musk ox left the circle and started prancing about, and all the others followed. It looked like a game of follow the leader. This behavior was stunning in that it seemed to have absolutely no survival value and was a bit risky.

Risk appears to be part of the pleasure and challenge of play. In play with friends, I love fast skiing from my soul and diving into awesome waves just for the sensual exhilaration of it. Because play *is built into our genes, the rewards of play must be greater and more* important for survival than the risks.[3]

We are finding that play is as important as food and sleep for the developmental processes of animals, especially humans. It may actually be our most important survival behavior, eliciting heart coherence, touch, movement, and the all-important sense of belonging.

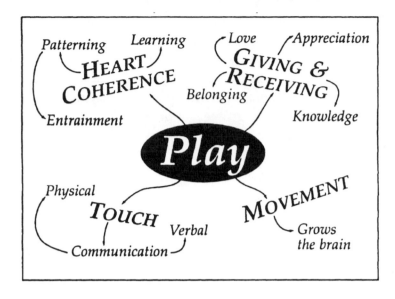

Figure 9.1: Aspects of Play

BILL OF RIGHTS FOR PLAY

All Players are equal or can be made so.
Novelty is more fun than repetition.
Rules are negotiable from moment to moment.
Risk in pursuit of play is worth it.
The best play is beautiful and elegant.
The purpose of playing is to play, nothing more.

—JOSEPH W. MEEKER [4,5]

Complex play doesn't seem to occur in fish, amphibians, or reptiles. These animals appear to be hard-wired into a format of survival/instinct reactions. Basically, if you're a reptile you run away from something bigger than you; you mate with something the same size, and eat anything smaller than you. You certainly don't play with it!

Apparently, play demands two characteristics in the players: 1) warm-bloodedness and 2) a complex, highly integrated brain with the capacity to dream. Dreaming comes from the limbic system, which emotionally structures our world and formulates our imagination.[6]

Warm-bloodedness provides the surplus energy needed for play. Since our metabolism keeps our body temperature constant, we don't need to shut down when it's cold (hibernate) or hot (find shade). Our extensive fat storage, which both insulates and provides energy, and our insulative hair covering help to protect and maintain our energy for play.

In humans, the most playful of all animals, play emerges within a secure, warm, and supportive environment, where parental involvement is abundant. The environment must be free from hunger, danger, and deprivation.[7] Prolonged parenting in birds and especially mammals, provides the needed protection, as well as the food necessary to free up energy for play.

Playful creatures have masses of neurons in their complex brains devoted strictly to the generation of rough-and-tumble play. These distinct neural systems are located in projection areas of the thalamus and specific nuclei (parafascicular complex and posterior thalamic nuclei) in the partietal lobe of the cortex. They are linked directly to body sensations, movement, and information processing within the cerebellum, thalamus, and cortex.[8] Play impulses originate in the brain and don't need to be learned.[9]

Information chemicals (neuropeptides, hormones, etc) in our bodies also affect play impulses. Certain chemicals are especially effective in arousing play (acetylcholine, glutamate, and opiods), while others reduce playful impulses (serotonin, adrenalin and GABA).[10] When we play, our brains release dopamine, a chemical that induces elation and excitement and makes it possible for us to easily coordinate our actions. Dopamine orchestrates nerve net development and alignment all over the brain. In people labeled hyperactive or ADHD and with Parkinson's disease, dopamine levels are low. Thus play is an important deterrent to hyperactivity, learning difficulties and disease.[11]

Play must be crucial for the development of our huge brains and complex systems because we play more than any other animal and for a longer period of time. Neotany means: having child like features, which we humans exhibit throughout our lives. With our remarkably malleable nervous systems, we are always in a state of development. Being playful that long potentially allows us to continue to take risks, be impulsive, creative, flexible, and loving, coming up with new ideas and implementing them till we die.[12]

Play Entails All Our Senses

Play is the rich blending of senses and emotion (energy in motion) and the fertile ground for all learning. Over 80% of the nervous system is involved in processing or organizing the sensory input we get from our bodies and the world around us. Thus the brain is primarily a sensory processing machine with the sensual nature of play giving us the most direct access to that machine.[13]

Children who have the enriched environment of nature and the freedom to explore it are very fortunate. For the brain's sake, it should be the norm. Our touch receptors and brain thrive on diversity:

> *the solid pressure of a hug or someone next to us,*
> *the soft brush of grass against bare legs,*
> *rough bark on fingertips,*
> *the smooth velvet of a new leaf,*
> *the solid coldness of a rock,*
> *the breeze dancing our hair out of place,*
> *and the prickly tingle of a pine cone.*

Brandy Binder, a vibrant, intelligent, happy child, suddenly started having seizures at the age of 4. The seizures became so frequent (over 100/day) that she became totally incapacitated. The doctors attempted to stop the seizures first through drugs, then by excising a small area of the brain, but to no avail. They finally opted to remove the whole right hemisphere of Brandy's brain. The ensuing paralysis of the left side of her body was devastating to this child who loved to dance and run.

On the advice of one doctor, the family began to challenge her body and senses through physical therapy, lots of massage, music, reading to her, nature walks, and lots of play—totally enriching her environment. The results were miraculous. At the age of 14,

Brandy was a happy, bright, straight A student, who rode horses, hiked and even danced.[14]

I had the fortune to meet Brandy and her mother when she was 18. This beautiful, highly literate, almost physically perfect young woman had won two major art contests with her brilliant "right brained" paintings, had secured scholarships to universities, and intended to become a public speaker. Brandy has challenged neuroscience to rethink right brain function and the extraordinary power of movement and play.

Our systems thrive on rich sensory challenges. Encountering new cultures, as I have over the past 15 years in 29 countries, demanded that I be absolutely present, coming with the curiosity of a child, and ready to step out of my judgments and habitual ruts. Not only did it challenge all my senses, it left me wiser and more compassionate.

We need to live in our senses daily, doing things in different ways, like eating with the other hand or walking a different way or changing a routine. Sensory challenge helps us stay awake and activates the vestibular system so we maintain our body posture; this in turn helps us to sleep deeply. You can tell if a person is living from her senses; she is confident and enthusiastic about her life in a wondering, curious, child-like way. [15] I love being in the enthusiastic presence of Joseph Chilton Pearce, author of *The Magical Child*, because he exudes wonder and awe while embracing life so fully.

Our senses shut down in our hurried, incoherent society, as we go into survival mode and become easily fatigued and depressed. It's the embezzlement of our potential.[16] Mom, 96, is constantly taking risks to do new, novel things for the fun of it, and she doesn't look or act a day over 70. She has a young mind and a bright spirit. A study of Alzheimers disease done in the Netherlands showed that old committed couples that argued were less likely to get Alzheimers than those who didn't.[17] We were given each other and our siblings to challenge us, to spar and play with, for the fun and growth of it.

"Life is nothing if not an adventure."
—*Helen Keller*

Babies are always exploring new territory. Experience a baby exploring your face with all her senses – it's awesome and slobbery. To a baby, your face is a much more enriched environment than any toy you could give her. For the baby's sake and your own, put the toys away; bring on the pots and pans and whisks and measuring spoons and scrubbers. Clear the floor and roly-poly play, jump on the bed, climb on the couch, and explore the dog. Throw away the dishwasher, get an oilcloth apron and highchair, and let that child explore the sensuous world of soap bubbles, the slippery feel of dishes and forks and dish cloths.

Bring on the mud, sand, birdseed, seashells, sticks, cardboard boxes, and stand back to give room for exploration. Eat all kinds of food with your fingers along with your child, stimulating two of the most sensitive parts of your body, the fingertips and lips. Be totally aware of and celebrate everything you eat, its color, smell, texture, and delightful taste. Play with your food, stir or squeeze it into an unrecognizable paste and smear it on your body, especially your nose. These are all suggestions from my wondrous friend, teacher, and child development expert, Renate Wennekes. [18]

Our fear of dirt may prevent us from letting our children experience the whole sensory environment. Researchers are now saying that our squeaky clean, antiseptic environments have weakened our immune systems, resulting in increased allergies, asthma, and autoimmune diseases such as rheumatoid arthritis and the most severe type of diabetes. The immune system organizes itself through experience, so these diseases tend to develop when the immune system lacks practice fighting bacteria and viruses. [19]

Kids need contact, not with disease causing agents, but with innocuous microbes in the soil and untreated water, to give the immune system a workout. Children growing up in big families, or on farms, or children from families who avoid antibiotics and vaccinations are much less likely to develop allergies. [20] Even insect bites help fine-tune the immune system, making it stronger and more resistant to dangerous bites from infected insects. [21]

Play Entails Movement

Up until November 1998, I had been telling students that though we were constantly developing new nerve networks, it was doubtful whether new nerve cells developed after 6 months of age. We now know that growth of new nerve cells occurs until the day we die. As many as 60,000 new nerve cells per day grow in the hippocampus, the place where we start formulating memories from environmental input.[22]

Research on rats and mice show that an enriched environment, one that is large, has diverse toys and running wheels, and is shared with many other rodents they can explore and play with, is necessary for these new cells to form and remain healthy. The running wheels were the real stars, causing the most cell growth, even in very old rats and mice.[23,24]

The body grows the brain through movement with the vestibular system being the unifying factor. The vestibular system, mainly made up of the semicircular canals, utricles and saccules, cerebellum, and Reticular Activating System, connects with all the movement centers in the brain as well as all our muscles, thus priming the entire nervous system to function optimally. The connections between the cerebellum and the hippocampus are extensive, explaining why movement is so important to nerve growth. The vestibular system organizes our understanding of gravity. To know our relationship to the earth is more compelling than our need for food, touch, or even the mother-child bond.[25]

Watch a baby roll over or a child jump for joy, and you will notice a spiral pattern. It's the same spiral we see in the double helix of the DNA, the spiral growth in plants, or the spiral in the currents of the ocean that scientists call the Archemedian twist.[26] This spiral movement is tied directly to the vestibular system, waking up the brain and facilitating all incoming sensory information. Autistic children are missing these normal spiral movements. Philip Teitelbaum's study showed that normal children learn to roll over at about 3 months old, using a corkscrew (spiral) motion while autistic babies exhibit no such movement. Their movements tend to be asymmetrical and unbalanced, indications that the vestibular system has not developed properly.[27]

Swinging and spinning is essential to development. The playground of the one and only school in Havelock, Iowa, had a merry-go-round like none other in the world. It consisted of a circular wooden bench, suspended from a big central 8 foot high pole by metal guy wires, so it hung freely, and boy could it spin! Kids would pile on en mass and hold on tight while other kids would run around the outside, propelling it to greater and greater speeds. It was awesome!

Now, I am hard pressed to find merry-go-rounds on any playground, and swings are even becoming rare. Safety seems to be the concern, but it might just leave us with clumsy, accident-prone kids that haven't done enough balanced movements to develop their vestibular systems. Currently, less than 15% of Americans get regular exercise, less than 30% of school children have daily physical education, and whole areas like Atlanta, Georgia, have gotten rid of recess. These statistics support a worry of the American Academy of Pediatrics, that fewer than half of all school children get enough exercise to develop healthy hearts and lungs. This affects the amount of oxygen the brain and muscles receive and leaves children uncoordinated. In order to develop coordination, children must be allowed to spin and explore gravity through swings, merry-go-rounds, climbing trees, rolling down hills, walking on fences, jumping on beds, and all those wonderful, risky things we did as kids. I love to see kids being swung around by parents where both parent and child are getting vestibular activation.

We as adults have a harder time with spinning because at puberty the fluid in the semi-circular canals thickens, so we tend to get dizzier faster and stay dizzy longer. But I have found that when I spin on a regular basis, I don't get dizzy, especially if I do some Brain Gym® before and after and the spinning wakes up my brain, assists coordination and puts me back in the child state of joy.[28]

Recently I have come across many schools that have added labyrinths to their playgrounds. These spiral structures, traced back over 3500 years to the Island of Crete, are thought to balance the two hemispheres of the brain. The equal number of left and right turns, along with geometric regularity, has been found to establish a balanced (coherent) pattern for those who walk it. Walking through the spiral pattern has been shown to greatly help children labeled ADHD, autistic, dyslexic and emotionally handicapped. The labyrinth requires increased focus, attentiveness, and balance just to walk, skip, or run through it. This calm, focused attention is reported to stay with the child during cognitive learning tasks. Some added advantages of the labyrinth for struggling students include:

1. Reaching the center is assured, so there is no failure—you can't do it wrong.
2. Walking the labyrinth is more about the journey than the destination, being more than doing.
3. The entire labyrinth is visible to the person as they walk it so there is no stress.[29]

Figure 9.2: Crete Labyrinth

Figure 9.3: Labyrinth at Palm Bay Elementary, Palm Bay Florida

Play Entails Touch and Laughter

*"Like clay that has been left out, we become rigid, hard and brittle if
we are left untouched. Through touch of child's play we, like clay,
become delightfully pliable stuff – well made, good to handle and to
live with, and above all alive with use."*
—O. Fred Donaldson, *Playing By Heart*

The skin is our largest sense organ and the first to meet our environment directly. It is like a space suit, equipped to check out all the diverse senses around us through a rich assortment of nerve endings that pick up light touch, pressure, pain, heat, cold, and vibrational patterns. There are even protective touch receptors around our hair follicles, which respond to sound and air vibrations moving across the body. They literally tell us where our body ends and space begins.[30] Already at birth, touch provides safety and comfort after separation from the mother and on into later life, as we experience subsequent separations or need for connection.

Touching the skin sends messages to the brain that stimulates the production of oxytocin and endorphins. Oxytocin promotes the bonding between the mother and baby, and endorphins produce a sense of well being at birth.[31] Chinese traditional hospitals mandate that the mother and baby must be skin to skin for the first half-hour after birth to assure bonding and to bring health to the child throughout life.

In Bali, people make a poltice of garlic and coconut oil that they rub on the newborn, lovingly but with rough pressure, to wake up the baby's senses and protect it from evil. The babies I saw loved it, and became calm, alert, and happy children.

Early touch leads to a strong immune system, better weight gain, and permanent sensitivity of the hypothalamus, resulting in reduced levels of stress hormones and a calm baby. With premature babies, 15 minutes of massage three times daily brings about a 45% increase in weight gain.[32] As the babies mature, the levels of oxytocin and endorphins from touch, continue to give a sense of being loved and produces self-assured, self-directed, loving people.[33]

Touch is so important to the safety and the initial development of the child that without it, the child's brain may not develop well, and he or she may die.[34] When our need for touch is not met, our stress increases, bringing on the cascade of cortisol and adrenalin. Children without touch will attempt to get that need met through self-stimulation of hitting, biting or pinching themselves or others.

Touch is the strongest anchor in validating who we are. It is ten times more important than verbal or emotional contact.[35] Humans will do anything for touch. We start by doing what we think other people want, just for a pat. If that doesn't work, we will do just the opposite to be hit or spanked, which is also touch. In either case we are getting the life sustaining touch we need for survival.[36] We often touch children and adults when they are acting in a negative, dis-empowering way, which tends to anchor that action. A better ploy would be to catch them "being good" or doing something empowering and then touch them.

In our family, dad was the cuddler. I would run to the end of the block to meet him after work so he would carry me home on his shoulders. I would crawl into his lap everytime I got the chance. And he would put his arm around my shoulders when I needed that safety. Separation from that touch was part of the great wounding that occurred when I started into puberty. After working with a psychotherapist, I now understand the incest fear, which occurs commonly in fathers as their daughters mature. In order to handle the incest fear, they pull away, leaving their daughters wondering what they did wrong to lose dad's affection.

This lack of touch has been compounded in our society with fears around *how to touch*. Teachers are even asked not to touch their students, and homophobia has inhibited friends from hugging. Since rough and tumble play is so steeped in touch, this important growth activity has decreased between children and between parents and children. Thus we have become a society of people feeling separate from each other.

Touch gives us the sense of belonging and safety to explore and learn from our life. Touch precedes both hearing and vision as our primary channel for learning.[37] All touch stimulates the production of NGF (nerve growth factor), which stimulates dendritic growth on the neurons throughout the body, and keeps the new nerve cells and dendritic connections healthy. Traditional Chinese Medicine recognizes touch by saying; "The sense of touch is dependent on the Heart and Mind, as this is responsible for the cognition and organization of external stimuli sensations."[38] The Institute of HeartMath showed that when people touch, there is transference of the electromagnetic energy of the heart of one person which affects the brain waves of the other person. If I have a coherent heart rate variability (HRV) pattern and reach out to hold the hand of another person, that person's brain waves will become coherent as well.[39]

Touch also is the key to provoking play. Friendly tickling is one of the easiest ways to provoke first a smile in response to social interaction, starting at about 4 months of age, and laughter in young children as early as six months of age.[40] Mammals appear to have "play skin" or "tickle skin", with specialized receptors sending information to specific parts of the brain that communicate playful intentions between animals. Human "tickle skin" is located at the back of the neck and around the rib cage, where it is easiest to tickle people and get them into a playful mood.[41] Tickling is a natural invitation to play, but when it turns uncomfortable or malicious, it can become an attack or a means of control and no longer part of play.

Laughter is the hallmark of play in action. Scientifically, it is merely a projectile respiratory movement with no apparent function, other than to let others know of our happy social mood[42]. Laughter appears to be genetic because even blind and deaf children laugh.[43] The 80 muscles that make up our face control blood flow to the brain. The muscles that contract during laughter raise the blood flow to the brain, creating a feeling of joy. Laughing also increases the brain's temperature, protecting it from disease organisms and affecting the release of neurotransmitters that influence emotions. Laughter can raise heart rate as much as aerobic exercise and increase one's tolerance to pain and discomfort. When we consciously or unconsciously reproduce the facial expression of another, especially laughter, we have a similar emotional feeling, a state of empathy.[44]

Neurologically, laughing and crying both come from the brain stem and are intimately connected. This may explain why I cry when I am overjoyed or touched deeply by something that makes me feel connected. And it explains those instances where we laugh so hard we cry.[45]

"Laughter is the quintessential human social signal.
It solidifies relationships and pulls people into the fold."
—*Albert Provine*[46]

Play Is a Social Investment

"Play is the work of children."
—*Ashley Montigue*

Play allows us to be effectively assimilated into the structure of our society.[47] A playful life with full and free play in childhood, continuing throughout adulthood, correlates with good social skills and flexibility, physical health, curiosity, and innovativeness.[48] Dorothy and Jerome Singer, child psychologists at Yale University, found that kids who initiate imaginative play show leadership skills in school. They cooperate more with other children and are less likely to antagonize and intimidate others.[49] Play helps to stitch individuals into the social fabric, which is the staging ground for their lives.[50]

In play, we learn about the world and how to be in it in a cooperative, co-creative way. Our play face lets the other player know there is trust and teaches us to accurately read facial cues in our social interactions. The play of chase and "tag" helps to keep things equal where the chased and chaser are constantly shifting, sharing power, and relinquishing authority. This gives children and later adults the ability to work in unison with each other.[51] In the game of chase, the child being chased will constantly look at the chaser to make sure the other is still there, still connected, with neither child wanting to break the connection.

Wrestling and rough and tumble play provide the solid touch so important to a sense of being in our bodies and belonging. It helps us develop balance and focus. It also gives us an acute awareness of where others are in relationship to ourselves. Children who haven't rough and tumbled a lot tend to be clumsy and unaware of other people's space as they bump into them or step on them unintentionally. These children struggle with staying present with others or focused for learning because they aren't solidly in their bodies.

Follow the leader lets us explore new ways to do things, thus expanding our imagination. It facilitates our understanding of how to organize our ideas to be easily followed. It also accommodates the give and take of leadership, honoring each person's special talents and ideas.

Tickling, wrestling, and chasing involve negotiation, provide lessons in getting along with others, and require the restraint of aggressive impulses. These abilities help to safeguard and maintain the alliances that are needed in adulthood.[52] In true play, everyone is relaxed and aware of where others are, so they roll and connect in a way that assures no one gets hurt. If someone gets hurt, it isn't play.

The picture on the following page shows children at the Wald Kindergarten in Kirtzarten, Germany, learning cooperation and creativity through play. These 3 – 5 year old children decided to build a house, so three of them found a very large building stick. In moments, two others had joined them in cooperation. Imagination, agility, cooperation, and self-confidence are the side effects of healthy play. Early experiences of play are crucial for anchoring our spirit and bringing us home to ourselves, in order to be adept at social interactions and weather the storms we will inevitably face throughout our lives.[53]

Play and Creativity

Play develops the patterns and flexibility to live without anxiety in a world that continuously presents us with unique challenges and ambiguity, so we can remain plastic and creative.[54]
                                        —*Paul McLean*

As we develop, play lays the groundwork for creative thinking in adulthood as our cognitively focused higher brain areas add more and more complexity.[55] With more complexity and diversity, our play leads to the creative art of play, playing with ideas, words, music, visual art, and movement. Art is one of the greatest rewards of risking to play.

"True play is the ability to play with reality. True play drives imagination, gives resiliency, flexibility, endurance and the capacity to forego immediate reward on behalf of long-term strategies". [56]
—Joseph Chilton Pearce

Figure 9.4: Learning cooperation through play.

Play encourages us to test the perimeters of our knowledge and change the way we and our society sees the world. It's through the play of great artists like Einstein, Leonardo DeVinci, Thoreau, and Mozart that major paradigms (societal beliefs) have been changed. It's interesting that the term poet means change maker.

"Art and play sometimes takes risks that threaten the tidiness that civilization values so highly. They are sources of new experience and they encourage change, so they worry people who like things to stay put and be obedient. They are full of surprises."
—*Joseph W. Meeker*[57]

Play, as our most profound change agent, is essential to our self- understanding and growth. Perhaps the "fountain of youth" exists in our remaining mentally and physically playful throughout our lives, tapping our creativity and wonder rather than artificially attempting to extend longevity.

Consequences of No Play

At all ages, the disappearance of play from our lives is usually experienced as a significant loss. Jay Teitel, in an article on play, states that "adults have not only abducted play from kids, but have returned it to kids in adulterated form, driven by fear and perfection". Play seems to have become highly structured, over-planned, competitive sports play that starts very early with parent/coach orchestrated little league, competitive physical education programs, computer games, or play with toys that intrude on imagination, the very soul of kids' play. These can easily turn into work rather than play.

We tend to be overprotective, not trusting our children's power, seeing them as potential victims instead of survivors. "Powerful play requires powerful and independent players." Powerful play gives children the freedom to educate themselves in the ways of the world, to truly know something by inventing it and to relate deeply with others.[58]

To understand the rewards of play, it helps to see how lack of play inhibits growth and development. When we don't play regularly throughout our lives, our social behavior as well as our health is compromised. Play begins with the mother-child connection. When baby monkeys were isolated from their mothers at birth, they missed all the developmental play that occurs through mother/baby interaction. Without play and closeness, they lived in a perpetual state of fear and withdrawal. They rocked back and forth (to get the movement they needed) or bit themselves (for the sensory stimulation), and became violent when placed with other monkeys.[59]

Prescott studied indigenous cultures that touched and carried their babies on their bodies all day as opposed to those that did not. Where infants were carried on the bodies of their mothers, the levels of violence in the culture were low (e.g. Maori, Papago, Balinese). In cultures where babies were't carried, the violence levels were high (Comanches, Masai, Thonga).[60]

Without touch, movement and play, children develop brain abnormalities associated with violence, hallucinations, and schizophrenia.[61] Isolation inhibits large areas of the brain from developing normally: the sensory system of the cerebellum that controls movement and balance, the integrative somesthetic area in the cerebrum for touch, and the system that controls affection which is directly linked to touch and movement. Children who miss play and touch have 20 – 50% smaller brains.[62]

Violent, antisocial men and young murderers tend to have had controlling parents, profound abuse as children, and normal play behavior virtually absent throughout their lives.[63] Play and the survival-based systems in the brain are separate from each other. Many of these violent young men are on psychostimulants for depression. These stimulants prompt survival-based activities, adding to their already chronic stress state and disrupting any potential for play.[64] "The opposite of play is not work, its depression, separation and isolation".[65]

The twenty five-year-old murderer, Rene Spitz, experienced separation, isolation, and abuse in a play-less childhood. Though he was a good student, his lack of play led to depression, which also meant depression of his impulse control, leading to pathological violence.[66] The same is true for the boys that killed at Columbine High School. Following the Columbine shooting, a women from Pennsylvania put it this way: "Adults need to get the courage to ask: how did we come to raise children filled with fear and rage and loneliness? What can be said of a culture that forever puts the production and accumulation of meaningless material objects ahead of the spirits, hearts, and minds of its own children? Where are we as a people, how did we get here, and where do we want to go?"[67]

Play is the way we establish a sense of self, empathy, social altruism, and compassion. Play is a fairly dependable predictor of whether a society will be peaceful, affectionate, and cooperative.

"Culture is the handmaiden of our neurobiology, and without a proper environment for physical affections, a peaceful, harmonious society may not be possible".[68]

—James Prescott

A Play Day with Fred

Remembering how to play takes experiencing it first hand.[69] I was fortunate to be a student of and teach with O. Fred Donaldson. In his book, *Playing By Heart*, he talks of how children had been his teachers and mentors, and how the play patterns they exhibited were similar to those of wild animals at play.

In a "playshop" I taught with Fred, we started by experiencing the safety in touching ourselves, through a cat and mouse story, which activated sensory receptors on the hands, arms, legs, and face.[70] Laughter filled the room as the first letting go of play occurred. Then we did simple "push hand/push arm" aikido activities with partners, learning to touch in a safe, non-aggressive, non-competitive way, a flow of giving and receiving, of being present and connected.[71,72]

We moved to sitting back to back on the floor, again using equal pressure and energy against each other, flowing, yielding and giving. Solid pressure on our backs gives us the feeling of being in our bodies and belonging. Pressure on the back helps to grow and mature nerves originating from the spine out to all the other areas of the body in segments called dermatomes. The more we touch a baby or child's back, the more developed will be their sensory system. When I work with children who are tactilely defensive and hyperactive, I have them roll up in a blanket like a "hot dog", giving them the safety of being swaddled. Then I roll a medium sized beach ball along their backs starting with light and moving to firm pressure, which both relaxes and stimulates the maturation of nerve endings past their sensitivity.[73]

When we were sufficiently primed to engage fully; the playground area was assigned, the rules of no standing up, no grabbing, or tickling were established; and we got onto our hands and knees and began to "Play" with each other. It was awkward, and fun, and warm, and solid, and we rediscovered how to roll on each other and with each other. Laughter and joy filled the space as we moved from playmate to playmate and then to the puppy pile in the middle where we experienced wondrous, secure pressure on the body. The middle was where everyone wanted to be. Then in joyful exhaustion, we lay across each other, an arm here, a leg there, catching our breath in the safe space of another. There were no controlling or sexual overtones; we were just kids again, without separate bodies, or lives or hearts. We all belonged and felt solid.

The next day, Fred went to Cherokee Shaner's fifth grade classroom to demonstrate how he plays with children. At first, the kids were interested, but tentative. After Fred had played with each child who volunteered, everyone was ready to be a part of the connectedness they were feeling, even as voyeurs. As they jumped on his back, he gently cradled them forward into an honest cuddle before he set them down for the next tactic.

We watched in wonder and joy—the beauty of children moving past their violent, TV models of aggression to playfully attacking Fred just to be cuddled. One boy, who hadn't spoken the whole year, piped up and asked Fred how tall he was. Cherokee and the students stopped in rapt amazement at the transformation in this once silent child.

We also visited a special education class of five to eight year olds. After Fred had played with each child on the lawn, he invited the adults to join in. Oh what joy, what absolute belonging I felt, rolling down a grassy slope with my tiny, 6 year old playmate cupped in my arms and me in hers, no perception of age or size. At the end, we all lay there laughing and panting, solid and safe with

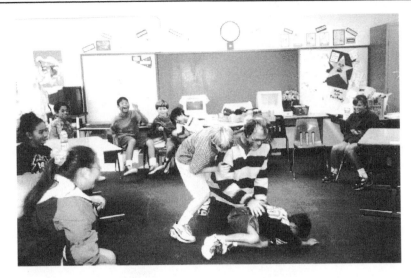

Figure 9.5: Play with Fred in Cherokee Shaner's fifth Grade Classroom, Hawaii

each other. The smile didn't leave my face, and the enthusiasm and focus for schoolwork remained with the children for days.

How do you explain to parents, teachers, administrators, and health professionals, the exquisite feeling of real play? I don't know other than to have people experience it as I did. Play, even imaginative physical play, is now an integral part of all my workshops. Parents, elementary teachers and some brave intermediate and high school teachers take it into the classroom to the delight of everyone involved.

So, I invite you to put down this book, go find a playmate, get down on the rug, grass, or whatever and play, right now, for the belonging of it.

CHAPTER TEN

How to Educate —
the Wald Kindergarten

"The real voyage of discovery consists not of seeking new landscapes, but in having new eyes."

—Marcel Proust

I strongly believe that play and its benefits should continue right into the educational curriculum. Play deeply anchors our ability to relate to others, have empathy, set boundaries, creatively solve problems, and learn optimally.

In the fall of 1998, I had a day free while in Southern Germany and happened to walk into the Black Forest, only to find, there before me, a group of little "gnomes" all playing without visible adult supervision. It was a preschool developed in Denmark called the Wald (forest) Kindergarten.[1] Over twenty three to six year old children attended this school five days a week. Of the five hours each day, three to four were spent outside in the forest learning from each other and the forest with its diverse seasonal changes and moods.

Games, alone or with playmates, emerged like raindrops from a moisture-laden cloud. Their unstructured play left room for all possibilities, and they hungrily experienced the options. There was lots of imagination, laughter, exploration, and discovery.

Some children climbed on logs across a stream, others wielded huge sticks that never once touched or hurt other children, while still others became enthralled by a flower, the patterns of pine needles, or the bark of a tree. There were times of active conversation when new finds were shared or as imaginative games emerged, were played, and dissipated. Children moved from group play to solitary play without fear of not being included.

Figure 10.1: Vestibular Development and Play at the Wald Kindergarten, Kirschzarten, Germany

Alone they would play, as songs floated from their concentrated lips. In a wide-eyed circle, the children experienced a lesson in steady beat, using rocks, sticks, dried stems of oak leaves, and pinecones. The rain lightly fell on them as part of the ambient atmosphere of their emerging forest band of natural instruments.

The rich multi-sensory environment was their unlimited playground. They had two adult consultants on hand to appreciate their discoveries, help them pick up big logs, hug them when needed, untangle their mittens, attend to the many layers of clothing so they could urinate, and elegantly support and facilitate their ability to learn.

There were few rules—the main one being "respect for all living beings". These children were learning all the rules for a successful life through their bodies, through their interactions with each other, and through their interactions with nature.

On the way to their forest shelter, each child was allowed his/her own pace, as the children independently climbed over rocks and around trees. A forest kindergarten I observed in Sweden had a mini-ropes course set up between trees. These two to six-year-olds balanced elegantly on the ropes, their vestibular systems and confidence well developed, aware of each other and ready to help in a tricky situation. Each caregiver was deeply loving and honestly amazed as each child taught about the glorious world she/he was exploring.

Figure 10.2: Ropes Course with 2 1/2-6 Year Olds, Forest Kindergarten, Stockholm, Sweden

To understand abstract ideas like math and reading we must have real, whole body experiences, that create a context. Nature and real experiences generate the questions and curiosity that motivate the learner to search and understand, at a deeper level. The first 5 years of life develop 90% of the child's ability to easily learn. The Wald Kindergarten elegantly sets up the learning apparatus for a lifetime.

In Denmark, this educational philosophy continues as children enter the Folkskol at age 7. A family-like structure remains intact as the teacher stays with the same group of students until they are 12 years old. The learning is experiential, cooperative, and often self-directed as students teach each other their discoveries. No testing occurs before age 14, accommodating the child's own pace and leaving each free to gain deep understanding, rather than piece-meal or "drill and kill" low level skills. This educational structure naturally creates social/environmental understanding, beginning with children teaching each other and culminating with cognitive skills which assure motivated life-long learners.[2,3,4]

Often in the U.S. education has been treated as a separate entity from play, the home and family. Our wonderfully diverse children, from different backgrounds and learning styles, are immersed for a period of time, in a standardized, fairly homogenous curriculum, that relegates play to a 20 minute segment in the morning, during lunch, and sometimes not at all. The child's physiology is often not ready to handle reading and printing, and the lessons are often not relevant to his/her world. With continuous homework, tests, and evaluation, the educational setting becomes stressful, devoid of curiosity or imagination, and the full potential of learning.

During Jim's and my separation and divorce, Breeze was still expected to perform in an educational setting as if her world were not being pulled apart at the seams. Her fears of losing one or both of us disturbed every waking moment of her life, but she was still supposed to learn to read and spell well. The deep lessons of family dynamics were glossed over in lieu of learning to add and subtract. Nothing in school dealt with the context of her life, and she floundered, not having a reference point. Constant drills and tests to somehow assess her intelligence superseded self-exploration and discovery. Breeze was learning huge lessons that weren't acknowledged because a scheduled curriculum needed to be met. With Breeze's stress, lack of focus, and natural kinesthetic bent, the counselor labeled her ADHD. Somehow we sidestepped the "treatment" and she went on, drug free, to become the perfectly wonderful person she is today.

Since school is deemed our authority on intelligence and learning, a person's self concepts are often influenced by the school labels they receive. In 1997, in the U.S. alone, 7.5 million children were labeled developmentally delayed as compared to 4.8 million in 1991. Every week, 15,000 American school children are being referred for assessment, with up to 80% of all school children considered to have some learning disability.[5] Learning is our most natural state, so when 80% of children are considered learning disabled, it's time to change our paradigm.

Child development experts agree that the only thing shown to optimize a child's intellectual potential is a secure, trusting relationship with their parents.[6, 7, 8] With our current "culture of neglect,"[9] working parents have little time for exploration, cuddling, interactive communication, and play with their children. The electronic babysitter (TV, computer, etc.) takes over, leaving the child without healthy models of how to govern themselves personally and socially in lieu of a sitcom humanity that lacks honoring and safety.[10] With the lack of a safe emotional home environment, rich in coherent human interactions, where children feel a sense of personal power and optimism about their future, they are left disconnected and fearful. This leads to learning difficulties and stressed out behavior.[11]

Stresses of the Cookie-Cutter Curriculum

"It surprises me how our culture can destroy curiosity in the most curious of all animals—human beings."
—Paul McLean[12]

When a child feels secure, connected, and coherent, the system is geared to grow a perfect human with an innate tendency and drive to learn. That same drive has the potential to grow exquisitely unique individuals endowed with special gifts that, if mined, can enrich and expand everybody's wisdom and life. And yet our current preoccupation with success has led us to push our children and ourselves to fit cookie-cutter molds that limit the perfection and gifts we possess.

Our current education system was set up to supply workers for a competitive, industrial, information-based society following WWII. However, it is becoming obvious that it doesn't fit what corporations want in today's workforce.

According to a study done by the National Learning Foundation, top American corporations want an agile workforce made of flexible, curious/creative, cooperative collaborators, who are altruistically motivated, aesthetically aware, reflective in their thinking, ambiguity tolerant and risk-takers. These are all traits that can only exist in a safe environment which empowers us to be authentically ourselves. Literacy, numeracy, and communication are still necessary, but only in the context of these other characteristics.[13]

Why is there now a demand for an agile workforce instead of one that follows instructions and is obedient, conforming, and competitive? A large number of the jobs available today didn't exist ten years ago. Corporations want inventive, curious people that can cooperate and take risks to come up with the work of the future, the new jobs for the next ten years. They want people who are authentic and deeply involved in life-long learning.

Dr. Lechleitner, professor of zoology, had a sign hanging over his door. Aside from his brilliant lectures and great sense of humor, that sign convinced me to pick him as my graduate advisor. It read: "If I have only made it possible for you to get a job, then I apologize. If I have given you a sense of curiosity and wonder about yourself and the world, then I have succeeded." Corporations are now catching up to Dr. Lechleitner though they may have more interest in creativity and productivity than wonder.

The Prime Minister of Singapore, one of the most economically successful countries in the world, has mandated total educational reform to develop a creative, agile workforce. Singapore has awakened to the fact that pushing children at the age of 3 to sit still and learn to read, and pressuring them to get high grades all through school, is not working. It is producing a generation of myopic people that can replicate anything, but who lack imagination, creativity, or the willingness to take the risks necessary to come up with new ideas.

In talking with parents and teachers in Singapore, I found their lives revolved around their child's education. Children would go to tutors before and after school with many hours of homework to complete before bedtime. Parents would stay home from work to quiz children during test week. The emphasis on competition and cognitive skills left no time for play, and parents found themselves applying great pressure to teachers and themselves to make their child succeed. It was shocking that 85% of five-year-olds in Singapore needed glasses because of the strain on their undeveloped eyes.

We are doing much the same in the U.S. The eyes are important indicators of stress from too much close visual work such as reading at too early an age. Sometime between preschool/kindergarten and high school, up to 50 percent of kids in the U.S. become myopic.[14]

Breeze and I observed this competitive tension for early learning when we taught a course in Singapore to adults (mainly business people) that included a lot of play. We talked about the importance of play for brain development and learning. We also discussed the importance of connecting with, exploring and seeing the wonders of life through the innocent eyes and body of a child. We then gave the participants "toys" to play with; streamers, pinwheels, slinkeys, bubbles, and objects from nature like seashells, seedpods, interesting pieces of wood, and a rich mixture of flowers and leaves so abundant in Singapore.

What happened next astounded both Breeze and I. It was an assault rather than play. It was as if they were compelled to "play" faster, harder, and better than anyone else. They frantically swirled the streamers, slinkys, and pinwheels causing them to become distorted or break. They took apart or crushed the delicate flowers, leaves, seedpods, and wood without even looking at them. And they had a surreal competition around who could blow the most bubbles—never stopping to notice their beauty. There was no exploration, just hard driving and competitive doing. In the ensuing discussion, the participants realized they didn't know how to play.

Over the next few days of the course, profound insights emerged. They all started to remember sweet, happy moments of play as children—free spirited and joyful. The play during the course became more peaceful, beautiful, exhilarating as their wondrous child natures emerged past the business suits. They also had the sobering realization that because of the high-pressured educational experiment of the past 20 years, their children didn't really know how to naturally play either, or learn for that matter. The price to society was a wasteland of conformity and a lack of passion, creativity and gentleness at home.

This wasteland of conformity shows up in studies such as Karen Arnold did with valedictorians in Illinois. These hard working, persistent, school centered, best students, considered the cream of the crop, all fit into the category of "conformists". They were very aware of and willing to abide by all the rules of the system. She made an interesting comment that "conventional good students tend to wind up as conventional successes" and went on to point out that the world's truly creative people were not conventionally good students, such as Thomas Edison, Ernest Hemingway, Albert Einstein, and even Bill Gates.[15]

I see more and more rebellious, unmotivated students and schools basing their curriculum around standardized testing programs that focus on literacy and numeracy. We so want our children to "succeed" that we push them into molds that focus on a narrow band of reality, and do it way too early. We encourage lots of homework to the exclusion of play, down time and deep human connection. Then we measure them by brutal standardized testing that leaves no room for the human spirit. If they don't fit the mold, acting out or not acting at all, we label and isolate and/or drug them into conformity.

We have ignored the research showing that homework has little or no effect on standardized test scores in grade school and is damaging to self-esteem and the desire to learn. Though homework is pointless in grade school, it was increased from 85 minutes/week in 1981 to 134 minutes/week in 1997. In Intermediate and High School, homework and testing can hone organizational skills, encourage time management, and develop the ability to learn autonomously. But in grade school, where the joy and passion of learning should be nurtured, it is causing burned out children with self-doubt and low self-esteem.[16]

The reading initiative which expects kindergarten children to read by the end of the year, standardized curricula, and testing in primary schools are causing what educators call "push down" academics. Thus children spend more time sitting still, listening to the teacher, and drilling on basics, with less time for physical and social skill development. Developmental experts across the country are saying that kids need more play rather than less, and lots of social interaction.[17,18]

"Grades, tests and class ranking kills off the love of learning and replaces it with superficial, grade-grubbing behavior."[19]
—Alfe Kohn

The Let's Give a Pill Culture

*"We are moving into an era where any quirk of a
personality is fair game for a drug".*
—*Time Magazine article on Troubled Kids*[20]

In dealing with children with learning disabled labels (ADHD, emotionally handicapped, etc) the answer, especially in the U.S., has been to give the child Ritalin or some comparable amphetamine. Time magazine noted that the percentage of children given prescriptions who were labeled ADHD jumped from 55% in 1989 to 75% in 1996 and is now over 90%.[21]

These amphetamines ("speed") do tend to calm the child, but in a way that perpetuates a dependency on these external drug supports.[22] Already in 1997, amphetamines were being used at the rate of 800,000 prescriptions written for children, some only five years old. By the year 2000, 15% of all school age children (8 million) were using Ritalin.[23] Ritalin production increased more than sevenfold between 1990 and 1998, with the U.S. consuming 90% of the Ritalin worldwide.[24, 25]

Concerns about Ritalin's widespread use brought together several hundred doctors, experts, and educators in November 1998 at the National Institute of Health in Bethesda, Md., to discuss this drug. The consensus was that for the great majority of children, taking Ritalin has very few benefits beyond simply masking the problems and controlling the behaviors. And even these effects disappear as soon as the drug wears off.[26] Participants expressed concern about the side effects, which include decreased appetite, insomnia, tics, and depression. It appeared to leave 43% of school children younger than 10 and 50% between the ages of 10 and 19 depressed.[27, 28]

Neither does Ritalin and comparable dexamphetamines appear to improve the child's long-term prospects regarding academic achievement, psychological well-being, or social behavior. Ritalin and other psycho stimulants can actually decrease our sensory-seeking behavior, thus decreasing our motivation to explore our world actively. Taking Ritalin for several days damages dopamine-rich cells in the brain area called the caudate as well as the habenula. The habenula maintains the connection to cells that produce serotonin and helps regulate dopamine transmission to the brain by slowing its release elsewhere.[29] Use of Ritalin causes dopamine to go elsewhere and seratonin to decrease: thus the body and focus slow down for a time. However, the motivational drive that makes us creative, unique, happy, curious individuals also decreases. The same occurs with other stimulant drug use, television, and video games, reducing our need to acquire stimulation through *our own* actions.[30]

Ritalin fails not only as a cure, but also as a reasonable interim solution.[31] The rise in children taking Ritalin has been correlated with a reduction in cases of natural remission of ADHD, which has gone from being the rule to the exception. Studies show how ADHD children turn into everyday, normal children under safe, pleasurable, sensory-rich conditions.[32]

Dr. Sidney Wolfe, director of Public Citizen's Health Research Group, feels that the risk of giving Ritalin or other drugs is just too great, if only because of the message it sends to children. In schools today we have whole programs devoted to teaching children to "Just say NO to Drugs" and yet by giving our children Ritalin, we are saying, "You are only OK if you are taking this drug". As always, we influence our children more by what we condone and do than what we say. These powerful psychoactive drugs come to be seen as no more harmful than vitamins.[33]

Eighty percent of the students taking the pills are boys. This fits the research showing boys need support for their emotional development and more movement for a longer period of time to fully develop the vestibular system and integrated frontal brain areas.[34, 35, 36, 37] On PET Scans, ADD and ADHD children have a smaller brain volume, particularly in the gray matter in the right frontal area having to do with movement and integration of ideas.[38] Two regions at the front of the corpus callosum that connect to parts of the brain involved in suppressing the impulse to fidget in class and activate proper production of dopamine are smaller.[39] When the research so strongly shows that integrated movement, supportive touch, and play grow brain areas necessary for increasing focus, and learning for a lifetime, without detrimental physical effects, why do we use harmful drugs?[40]

Ritalin doesn't help us take responsibility for the underlying causes, the hectic, incoherent home and school environments that so many children and adults face today. Is there a place for childhood and natural, relaxed learning in an anxious, over-technological Western Society worried about jobs, the marketplace, and children's chances of academic success?[41] It may be time to take back our health and power by consciously choosing to face and change the whole tenor of our lives, for our children and ourselves.

In Danish, Balinese and tribal African schools, I saw exuberant, focused, spirited, joyful, cooperative, respectful, non-competitive relaxed children. There was no inflexible agenda and no rush to fulfill a curriculum. No child was being graded or judged. There was no stress, no threat, no fear, nothing but that very moment in time and all the possibilities of learning. Hyperactivity and learning disabilities were scarce and accommodated through movement and a sense of belonging, leaving the children motivated to learn everything.

Educating with the Heart in Mind

Like the Danish schools, programs such as Susan Kovalik's ITI (Integrated Thematic Instruction) start with the absence of threat and nurturing belonging. ITI uses the Tribes work, created 30 years ago by Jeanne Gibbs as a Drug Prevention program. Students learn to know and honor each other as part of a tribe or classroom community. For any group to function well, each member must feel inclusion; thus cooperative learning groups become the norm.

Jeanne Gibbs points out that, if a kid doesn't feel inclusion, he will grab influence any way he can, thus disrupting the coherence of the group. For inclusion to occur, each person must 1) be acknowledged, 2) have their expectations be heard, and 3) feel they belong to the group. The developed community then actively 1) celebrates each achievement, 2) calls forth the personal gifts of each member, and 3) supports the group through challenges, including curriculum content and tests in school.[43]

Identity and life purpose need intimate community to develop; otherwise we don't have a true sense of our unique gifts or ourselves. Community is the enforcer of one's identity.[44] According to Breeze, if you don't have an audience in the theater, you don't exist as an actor. The same is true of life.

To expand pleasure, acknowledgment, and respect, programs like the ITI have instituted social skill trainings for the whole school community (janitors, cooks, office staff as well as teachers, administrators and students). The important skills of active listening, truthfulness, trustworthiness, no put-downs, and being your personal best, become habits for all members of the community. Because stress can occur when no solid perimeters or consequences are set, clear and humane "Lifeskills", that provide structure, boundaries and consequences are also a part of these programs. [45,46]

Rudolf Steiner, founder of Waldorf Education, felt that consistent structure was very necessary for the developing child up through the age of eleven, so she/he would have a solid framework of safety on which to explore and learn in her/his environment.[47] Students learn how to manage themselves and the consequences of making poor choices. If a child makes a poor choice, he is educated as to how it affects others and how to more lovingly and successfully obtain what he wants. This approach is far more effective than inhumane consequences, bribes, shaming, food or point rewards.[48]

The Love and Logic work gives excellent, compassionate, common sense ways to set boundaries, and administer humane consequences, while empowering the child, a must for any parent and/or educator.[49]

The "Lifeskills" concept really hit home for me. After the divorce, my sense of guilt at fracturing our family and having to work left me overly permissive with Breeze. Whatever she wanted I gave her and bowed to her every whim. When she overstepped her boundaries, I set consequences I never followed through on. I would physically be with her, but my mind was on my job or how to make ends meet or the confusion I felt about my life. She became a "bratty" child, unruly and unmanageable. Desperately wanting my own time, I relished the times when she would be invited to play with friends at their homes. Finally when a friend would not let her children play with Breeze and told me it was because Breeze was "spoiled", I was first shocked and then thankful for the guidance. I hadn't set boundaries and taught her choices to manage herself socially and personally with others.

With her behavior, Breeze was asking for the consistent boundaries that would make her safe. In our culture we tend to be lenient and permissive with children when they are young and need the safety of consistent boundaries and rules, and we clamp down on them when they get older and need to develop healthy independence. Breeze was also asking me to be totally there with her instead of just physically. A psychologist once told me that people only need 15 minutes of one-on-one, human connection each day, to feel safe. Children, especially, are aware of when we are not totally present; but so are our spouses, friends, other family members, and our world at large.

"A child should never be given a toy that has no purpose, or given actions to carry out which have no meaning. Nothing that one does with an infant ((child)) should be purposeless. If it is so, then it's whole life will be purposeless."
—*Hazrat Inyat Khan*

10.3: First Hand Experiences as Basis for Learning in the ITI (Integrated Thematic Instruction) Program

As Khan, Susan Kovalik believes all learning must be directly related to the child's real world. Each part of the curriculum starts out with a hands-on, in the field experience, out of which arise the questions and contexts that students will use to expand their knowledge. Nothing about the curriculum is superfluous, and every part is related directly to the interest of the child.

What changed the school failure dynamics for Breeze was her interest in theater and acting. We were blessed in Kona with an active community theater that encouraged and welcomed young people. The theater somehow made sense to her life, with its rich moving stories of people that misunderstood each other, loved deeply, made mistakes, and found the essence in life. The plays became healing for her as she started to put them into context with her own life.

Her two peak performances came as Helena in "Mid-Summer Night's Dream" and Emily in "Our Town". She was highly resistant to reading her social studies book, yet when the auditions were announced, Breeze got the Shakespeare text of "Mid-Summer Night's Dream" from the library, read the whole thing in one sitting, and spent hours telling me about the characters. These characters allowed her to finally laugh at her life's dramas (like Helena longing for love), realize the tenuous nature of relationships, and gain a deep sense from "Our Town" of what is most precious in life. It was contextual learning, and she was the director, choosing the curriculum that taught her what she was most interested in.

> *"We create the image and impression of who we are from the understanding we receive from others".*
>
> —*Becky Bailey*[42]

Learning begins in the home, actually in utero. It occurs when parents model being enthralled with the world, learning voraciously, and joyfully interacting with all the possibilities of life. In our hurried success driven society, parents work hard to give their children everything, but they miss what children need most: their parents, a deep sense of belonging, open communication, play, down time (daydreaming) and consistent humane rules and boundaries.

Without these, our children feel isolated and learning becomes secondary to survival. In the next chapter we will explore this in greater detail.

Loving teachers and parents who trust the child's innate altruism, empower them to make right choices, follow their truth, learn how to have healthy relationships, explore the wonder and beauty of the earth, and optimally learn.

CHAPTER ELEVEN

The Future of the Child Heart

"The love of God, unutterable and perfect, flows into a pure soul the way that light rushes into a transparent object. The more love that it finds, the more it gives itself; so that, as we grow clear and open, the more complete the joy of heaven is. And the more souls who resonate together, the greater the intensity of their love, and, mirror-like, each soul reflects the other."
—*Dante Alighieri (1265-1321) Purgatorio XV.67-75.*

The world needs Dante's insight now more than ever, to resonate from that coherent, altruistically present place where we realize our connection to, our impact on, and, the preciousness of all beings. A place to start is with the children of the world. Barbara Kingsolver[1] writes about being taken aback in Spain at the tangible respect and love people instantly show for children. People would stop on the street or anywhere to be absolutely present with and say wonderful things to her young daughter. I also saw this in Africa, as huge smiles would break over the faces of people when they saw a baby or child, followed by wonderful sounds and joyful touching. If a Balinese person heard someone yell at or spank a child, they would be mortified. Children are the most cherished gifts from heaven.

These cultures see the future in their children, honoring them to grow up healthy, happy, and connected so they will add to the culture and take loving care of the adults and society that raised them. Cherished children grow into cherished adults, embodying the greater intensity of love described by Dante.

In Western society, with our bid for independence within the nuclear family stronger than the embrace of an extended family, we often tend to isolate our love to our family. Childless couples often ignore children all together, seeing them as a nuisance or a threat to their peace of mind. This kind of shortsighted thinking isolates us from the core of our being, the rich, pleasurable human experiences that manifest a compassionate, altruistic global community. Our children, as the pilots of our future, will either grow up compassionate and loving to be our caregivers when we get old, run our services, teach us, enrich our world through wisdom, art and music, OR THEY WON'T.

At times I feel we are lost in intellectualism, technology, consumerism, and competition, a fracturing between the heart and brain. Our sense of inadequacy doesn't go away as we get older, and we act out, on the world's stage, what is unresolved in our psyche.[2] We take on the survival role of "lost child" described by Sharon Wigschneider-Cruze. In this state we lose touch with our emotions, trust and intimacy that connect us with our magnificence and that of others, while intellectualizing everything. In our mistrust of self and others, we set up rigid criteria of how another person or thing should operate to make us feel safe. The world and others become something to manipulate, harm, or feel victimized by.[3] In extreme cases, we become the boys at Columbine High School or the terrorists of the world.

According to Senator John Vasconcellos, we're coming into a new revolution at this time. The previous revolutions helped us order our lives to this point: gender equality, race equality, technology, ending the cold war, global economy, and the Internet.

The next revolution is the New Copernican Revolution, as described by Willis Harman, where we are moving from competition to collaboration. It is a revolution to regain our self-esteem, a positive sense of who we are, and compassionately facilitate and support that in others so we and our planet can heal. For this to happen fully, the key belief must be that "We are trustworthy, our children are trustworthy and others are trustworthy." A sense of altruism must permeate how we see others and how we teach our children.[4]

Decade of the Child Heart

The 1990's were deemed the decade of the brain, and science put much energy and focus on understanding this remarkable organ. Assigning the brain the role of master controller fit our linear, patriarchal, intellectual, non-emotional paradigm well.

But what if, as the ancient yogis, doctors of Traditional Chinese Medicine, and current researchers claim, the master controller is actually the holographic body, the intricate interplay of the heart, emotions, and brain. With our new understanding, perhaps we should deem the next decade, *THE DECADE OF THE CHILD HEART*. The Latin word for heart is "cor", the base word for courage, or "court" meaning the heart of the country, or the "core" of everything. I can envision the possibilities of a world of people who truly love and empower children, themselves and other adults. Our emphasis might be on community coherence and cooperation rather than commerce, competition and warfare. The decade of the Child Heart could be a period of understanding our universal connection, via vibrational patterns, to everything and everyone else. We might have to change our stance from being masters of the earth able to exploit it with our technology, to being protectors of our planet which is an energetic extension of ourselves and vital to our lives.

Children's success would no longer be measured by their performance on tests, early reading, or performing technological wonders on computers at ever-earlier ages. Children might be cherished and viewed as sacred entities, highly sensitive and sensible to vibrational patterns within and around them. We could join them in their discoveries of themselves and their world, thus expanding our knowledge of ourselves. There could be lots of play, curiosity, co-creativity, gratitude, and joy. We might recognize and honor the sacred gifts of all living beings, and judgment would be replaced by wonder at their beauty, diversity, and wisdom.

We might be open to exploring a vibrational reality far beyond the current reality we have honed, so shaped and limited to a miniscule portion of the vibrational spectrum. We might learn to easily access the non-local information field and work with all the creative minds, from every age group, to expand the possibilities of coherence in a worldwide energy web—inconceivable to our current technology.

We might even learn from the wisdom of the ancients, trusting cultures which gave the world its first technology as well as great works of art, music, and philosophy. At the center of these ancient cultural beliefs is the heart. The heart has always been the starting point for all yogic traditions and is the center of balance, the yin and yang, in Oriental traditions.

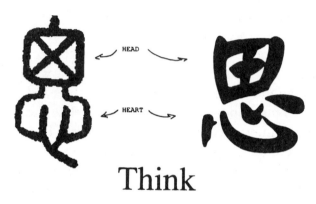

Think

Figure 11.1: Chinese Symbol for TO THINK

In Traditional Chinese Medicine, the Mind (Shen) = Heart, which is said to be the "residence" and governor of the mind. The Chinese characters for thought, thinking, and pensiveness all have the character for "Heart" as their radical. Thinking, consciousness, sleep, insight, memory, cognition, intelligence, wisdom, and ideas are all dependent on the heart. Intelligence is insight and reflection, raising self-knowledge and self-recognition above cognitive intelligence.[5] If the heart is strong, its owner will act wisely.[6,7]

These ancients may supply us with wisdom that could guide us out of the chaos we have bought into. When Marie Louis Van Franz of the Jungian Institute was asked, "Is there hope for humanity?" She answered: "I don't know, it is a matter of the heart." [8]

The Passionate, Emotional Child Heart

The heart has always been equated with our emotions, as in "glad heart", "broken heart", "bless her heart", etc. Much of Western society has believed that emotions were either superfluous, relegated to the instability of hormonal women, or a sign of pathological conditions. It is well condoned by our society to speak "ad nauseum" about the woes of the world, from many different angles, and to consider ourselves informed and intelligent by doing so. But when someone genuinely feels joy and elation, or deep sadness and anger, and expresses it, they are considered "Pollyanna", unrealistic, uninformed or simply "out of control".

With this stigma on emotions, we tend to discourage normal emotional development in our children. In the early stages of emotional development children are acutely aware of their parent's emotions and physically mimic them to learn. This shows up in gross, clumsy ways as temper-tantrums or overly enthusiastic excitement that we might label hyperactivity. If a child's emotional exploration is honored, the child learns how to responsibly feel and express emotions and to trust their bodies' messages, their gut/heart reaction, which research shows is usually right.[9] This development gifts the child/person with an enriched, passionate life and the ability to connect deeply and intimately with others and the world.

Emotions orchestrate every part of our reality, structuring our intelligence, our ability to do high-level formal reasoning, and create new and interesting things and ideas.[10] The emotions generated by the amygdala/heart complex in connection with the frontal lobes, provide insights that produce empathy, altruism, clear decisions and right action. Empathy is one of the most important emotions to develop within the structure of a loving home, neighborhood, society and global community. Empathy provides us with the mirror to become aware of our feelings and connect more intimately with ourselves through others. The more people receive empathy, the more "whole" and empathic they become and the more coherent is their brain function. More empathic children performed better on SAT, IQ and school achievement tests than did children that had not developed empathy.[11]

Immature, extreme emotions are on the rise in our society today. Larry Peters, an anthropologist, believes it has to do with lack of a strong family context and meaningful rites of passage. Rites of passage are an integral part of other cultures, allowing the whole family to regularly recognize and celebrate the child as an important, real person. He believes these extreme emotions are a means to communicate distress and "attempts at self-healing in a culture bereft of an integrative spiritual and ritualistic context."[12]

Mature emotions allow us compassion, altruism, empathy, and love.[13] To me, being in control means acknowledging and emotionally expressing, and celebrating in a responsible (responding) way, all the aspects of who I authentically am. As children (even in utero) we began perceiving the safety or threat of our world, assimilate a set of beliefs or thought patterns, and then build our reality. As we make a habit of coherence, we begin understanding what it means to be unlimited potential, connected deeply with everything, and life expands to a magnificent adventure in love.

A Reflection of Love

Paul Solamon tells about deciding to become a great healer. For his initial training his teacher had him get 5 tomato plants and keep them alive and healthy. He watered them faithfully and gave them plenty of sunlight. But, alas, all the tomato plants died. Undaunted, he got more tomato plants, cared for them, but they also died. After killing 15 tomato plants, he decided he didn't want to be a healer after all.[14]

In a plant store, several months later, he became intrigued with a small cactus garden. Reasoning that cacti were very hardy and hard to kill, he bought the garden and kept in the front entryway of his home. Everyday as he came into or left his home he found himself taking time to observe the cactus plants, noting their unique structures and how they had changed. His curiosity made him more their student than their caretaker. The cactus plants thrived and bloomed in this developing relationship. Paul had discovered that to become a healer wasn't necessarily about caring for and helping others. It was more about being fully present, curious, and appreciative of others.

Being curious and honestly seeing another person is the greatest gift we can give them and ourselves. Oxytocin, a pituitary hormone, vitally influences a person's ability to bond with others and forge close relationships.[15] Just looking into another person's eyes stimulates oxytocin release and accesses our frontal lobes, which are the seat of love, compassion and altruism.[16]

WITH THAT MOON LANGUAGE

Admit something: Everyone you see, you say to them,
"Love me."
Of course you do not do this out loud;
Otherwise, Someone would call the cops.
Still though, think about this,
This great pull in us to connect.
Why not become the one who lives with a full moon in each eye
That is always saying,
With that sweet moon Language,
What every other eye in this world
Is dying to Hear."

—Hafiz[7]

When we don't make eye contact, especially when a bond feels tenuous or we are not connected with our own completeness, we can be left feeling isolated and separate. When we don't look at our spouse or children when they speak, we break the connection. Seeing and affirming another sets up the trust and soul connection necessary for all of us to see our wonder.

I love the tradition in Sufi dancing, or Dances of Universal Peace, in which people look into another's eyes and sing to them. It "opens the heart" because it produces such a strong sense of peace, safety, and intimate connection. Many traditions use similar rituals to bring people together as a strong community.

The story is told of an Aikido master on his way home to the suburbs of Tokyo when a drunk got onto his subway car. The drunk was filthy, and in his oblivious state was yelling, swinging, kicking and hitting people as he came down the aisle. The Aikido expert, now standing at the end of the subway car, prepared himself to stop this drunk when suddenly an old man stood up between the aggressor and himself. The old man opened his arms, looked the aggressor in the eyes and said in a gentle voice, "Come here and talk with me." Instantly the aggressor stopped and began to sob, telling the old man of the struggles that had brought him to this point.[18] So simple and profound is the moment of love.

It may be time for us to look each other in the eyes, be totally present, and curious about this magnificent assembly of vibrational interference patterns across from us, this soul, this being on the way to becoming more authentic. Then we can open our arms to embrace the gifts this person brings to us through their unique understanding of our shared complex existence. It is a time to trust ourselves and others, to step out from behind our fears, lead with our child hearts, lay down our hectic way of life, play, sing and fully absorb all the wonder and beauty our current existence has to offer. Welcome to the "DECADE OF THE CHILD HEART" which makes possible fearless exploration into the universal field of intelligence, which many know as GOD.

NOTES

Chapter 1: The Importance of the Child Heart

[1] Spretnak, Charlene. 1997. *The Resurgence of the Real*. Addison Wesley.

[2] Pert, Candace. 2001. The Learning Brain Conference, August, 2001, Toronto, Canada.

[3] Prescott, James. 1997. Discovering the Intelligence of Play. Video. Touch the Future, TTFuture@aol.com.

[4] Chalmers, David. 1999. First person methods in the science of consciousness. *Consciousness Bulletin*, Fall 1999. Consciousness Studies, Dept. of Psychology, University of Arizona. p. 8 & 11.

[5] *World Book Dictionary*, 1983. Doubleday and Co., NY. p. 402.

[6] McCraty, Rollin, et. al. 1995. The Effects of Emotions on Short-Term Power Spectral Analysis of Heart Rate Variability. *American Journal of Cardiology*. 76(14):1089-1093.

[7] Akselrod S., D. Gordon, et. al. 1981. Power spectrum analysis of heart rate fluctuation: a quantitative probe of beat-to-beat cardiovascular control. Science. Vol 213:220-222.

[8] Pomeranz, B, J.B. Macaulay, & M.A. Caudill. 1985. Assessment of autonomic function in humans by heart rate spectral analysis. Am. J. Physiol. 248:H151-H158.

[9] Tiller, William, Rollin McCraty, Mike Atkinson. 1996. Cardiac Coherence: A new, noninvasive measure of autonomic nervous system order. Alternative Therapies, January 1996, Vol. 2, No. 1 p. 52.

[10] Hannaford, Carla. 1995. *Smart Moves, Why Learning is Not All In Your Head*. Arlington, VA: Great Ocean Pub. p. 147-149.

[11] Czikszentmihalyi, Mihaly. 1996. *Creativity; Flow and the Psychology of Discovery and Invention*. New York: Harper Collins. pp. 124-161.

[12] Hawkins, David R. 1995. *Power vs Force, The Hidden Determinants of Human Behavior*. Sedona, AZ: Veritas Publishing. p. 237.

[13] Rubic, Beverly, Ed. 1999. "The Interrelationship Between Mind and Matter," Temple University Symposium, Report of Group 2, Philadelphia. http://www.start.gr/user/symposia/group22.htm.

Chapter 2: Survival or Just Plain Stress?

[1] Odent, Michelle. 1986. *Primal Health, A Blueprint for Our Survival. Century*, Hutchinson, Ltd. p. 30.

[2] Elkind, David. 1988. *The Hurried Child: Growing Up Too Fast Too Soon*. Addison-Wesley, Pub., Reading, MA. p. 3.

[3] DeGrandpre, Richard. 1999. *Ritalin Nation: Rapid-Fire Culture and The Transformation of Human Consciousness.* W.W. Norton, NY. p. 30

[4] Mander, Jerry. 1978. *Four Arguments for the Elimination of Television.* Morrow, NY.

[5] Brahma Kumeris. 1998. Seeing Without Eyes. *Retreat*, Issue #8, Brahma Kumaris World Spiritual University. Leighton Printing, London. p. 27-28.

[6] Pearce, Joseph Chilton. 1992. *Evolution's End, Claiming the Potential of Our Intelligence.* Harper & Row, San Francisco. pp. 169-170.

[7] DeGrandpre, Richard. p. 22- 24.

[8] Ibid. p. 31

[9] R.B. Jacob, K.D. O'Leary, and C. Rosenblad. 1978. Formal and informal classroom settings: effects on hyperactivity. *Journal of Abnormal Child Psychology*, Vol. 6, 47-59.

[10] DeGrandpre, Richard. p. 32.

[11] Bloomfield, Harold. 1999. Tranquilizer use for heart disease and depression. Harvard Medical School Study.

[12] DeGrandpre, Richard. p. 25.

[13] Hannaford, Carla. 1995. *Smart Moves, Why learning Is Not All In Your Head.* Great Ocean Pub., Atlanta, GA. pp. 120-121.

[14] McEwen, Bruce, 1999. Review Article, *New England Journal of Medicine*, early 1999.

[15] Tortora, Gerard J. & Nicholas P. Anagnostakos. 1990. *Principles of Anatomy and Physiology (6TH Ed).* Harper & Row, NY. pp. 448-459.

[16] Ibid. Tortora and Anagnostakos. pp. 365-366.

[17] Jensen, M.C., Brant-Zawadsky, M.N., et al. 1994. Magnetic resonance imaging of the lumbar spine in people without back pain. *New England Journal of Medicine*, July, 14:331(2):69-73.

[18] Tortora and Anagnostakos. 1990. p. 418.

[19] Ibid, pp. 411-412.

[20] Ibid. p. 476.

[21] Marano, Hara Estroff. 1999. Depression: Beyond Serotonin. *Psychology Today*, March/April 1999. pp. 33-34.

[22] Ibid. pp. 72-73.

[23] Lee, John R. 1998. *The Indigo Children.* Warner Books, Boston, MA.

[24] Hannaford, Carla 1997. *The Dominance Factor.* Great Ocean Pub., Atlanta, GA.

[25] Reichal, Marcel. 1990. George Washington University, PET Scanner.

[26] DeFeo, P. 1989. Contribution of cortisol to glucose counterregulation in humans. *Am. J. of Physiology*, 257: E35-E42.

[27] Manolgas, S.C. 1979. Adrenal steroids and the dvelopment of osteoporosis in oophorectomized women. *Lancet*, 2:597.

[28] Michaelson, David. 1999. Depression; Beyond Seratonin. National Institute of Health. In: *Psychology Today*, March/April 1999. p. 74.

[29] Ebeling P., and V.A. Koivisto. 1994. Physiological importance of hydroepiandrosterone. *Lancet*, 343(8911): 1479-81.

[30] Blackburn, George. 1999. N. A. Association for the Study of Obesity.

[31] Diamond, Marian & Janet Hopson. 1998. *Magic Trees Of The Mind*. Dutton/ Penguin Group, NY. p. 80.

[32] Sapolsky, Robert. 1996."Why Stress Is Bad for Your Brain. *Science*, 273:749-450.

[33] Kempermann, Gerd, & Fred Gage. 1999. New Nerve Cells for The Adult Brain. In: *Scientific American*, May 1999. p. 48.

[34] DeFeo, P. E35-E42.

[35] McCraty, Rollin., Barrios-Choplin, B., Rozman, D. Atkinson, M., Watkin, A. 1998. The Impact of a New Emotional Self-Management Program on Stress, Emotions, Heart Rate Variability, DHEA and Cortisol. In: *Integrative Physiological and Behavioral Science*, 33(2):153-154.

[36] Musselman, Dominique. 1999. Depression: Beyond Serotonin. *Psychology Today*, March/April 1999. pp. 73-74.

[37] Leucken, Linda J. 1998. Childhood attachment and loss experiences affect adult cardiovascular and cortisol function. In: *Psychosomatic Medicine*, November/December, 60:765.

[38] Coplan, Jeremy D. et. al. 1996. Persistent elevations of cerebrospinal fluid concentrations of corticotropin-releasing factor in adult nonhuman primates exposed to early-life stressors: Implicatons for the pathophysiology of mood and anxiety disorders. *Proceedings of the National Academy of Sciences*. Feb. 20, 1996, vol.93(4); 1619-1623.

[39] Diamond, Marion. pp. 80-81.

[40] Namiki, M. 1994. Biological markers of aging. *Nippon Ronen Igakkai Zasshi*, 31:85-95.

[41] McCraty, Rollin. Director of Research, Institute of Heartmath.

Chapter 3: Depression - Sign of Our Times

[1] Marano, Hara Estroff. 1999. Depression: Beyond Serotonin. *Psychology Today*, March/April 1999. p. 32.

[2] Ornish, Dean. 1998. *Love And Survival: 8 Pathways to Intimacy and Health.*, Harper Collins, NY.

[3] Kendler, Kenneth, et al. 1993. The prediction of major depression in women: toward an integrated etiologic model. *Am. J. of Psychiatry*, 150:1139b-1148b.

[4] Leung, Kok Yuen. 1971. Traditional Chinese Teachings. College of Acupuncture course.

[5] DeQuervain, D.J., B. Roozendall and James McGaugh. 1998. Stress and glucocorticoids impair retrieval of long-term spatial memory. *Nature*, 394:787-790.

[6] Teeguarden, Iona M. 1996. *A Complete Guide to Acupressure.*: Japan Publications, Tokyo, Japan and New York.

[7] Marano, Hara Estroff. p. 34.

[8] Drevets, Wayne C. et al. 1992. A functional anatomical study of unipolar depression. *Journal of Neuroscience*. 12:3628-41.

[9] Bremner, J. Douglas. 1999. Does stress damage the brain? Biological Psychiatry, Vol. 45(7): 797-805.

[10] Drevets, Wayne C. et. al. 1997. Depression and the Prefrontal Lobes. *Nature*, April 24, 1997. In: *Science News*, vol. 151, April 26, 1997, p. 254.

[11] McEwen, Bruce and J. Douglas Bremner. 1999. *The American Journal of Psychiatry*, September, 1999.

[12] Redford, B. Williams, et al. 1997. Depression. *Science News*, July 1997, Vol 152. p. ll.

[13] Carrigan, Catherine. 1997. *Healing Depression*. Heartfire Books, Santa Fe, NM.

[14] Cohen, S. & T.A. Wills. 1985. Stress, social support, and the buffering hypothesis. *Psychological Bulletin*, 98, 310-357.

[15] Krackhards. D. 1994. The strength of strong ties: The importance of Philos in organizations. In: N. Nohria & R. Eccles (Eds.) *Networks And Organizations: Structure, Form And Action*. Harvard Business School Press, Boston, MA.

[16] Brody, G. H. 1990. Effects of television viewing on family interactions: An observational study. *Family Relations*, 29, 216-220 April.

[17] Andersen, R.E., C. J. Crespo, Bartlett, S. J, L. J. Cheskin, & M. Pratt. 1998. Relationship of physical activity and television watching with body weight and level of fatness among children. *Journal Of The American Medical Association*, 179, 938-942.

[18] Putnam, R. 1995. Bowling alone: America's declining social capital. *Journal Of Democracy*, 6, 65-78. January.

[19] Huston, A.C., et al. 1992. *Big World, Small Screen; The role of television in American Society*. University of Nebraska Press, Lincoln, NE.

[20] Kraut, Robert, Michael Patterson, Vicki Lundmark, Sara Kiesler, Tridas Mukopadhyay, and William Scherlis. 1998. Internet Paradox, A Social Technology That Reduces Social Involvement and Psychological Well-Being? *American Psychologist*, 53(9)1017-1031. September.

[21] DeAenlle, Conrad. 1999. Is All This Zippy Technology Actually Ruining our Lives? *International Herald Tribune*, October 8, 1999. p.9

[22] Fry, Christopher. 1951. *Three Plays: The firstborn, Thor with angels, A sleep of prisoners*. Oxford University Press, NY. p. 209.

[23] Middleton-Maz. J. 1999. Boiling Point; the high cost of unhealthy anger to individual and society. Deerfield Beach, FL: Health Communications, Inc.

[24] Niehoff, D. 1999. *The Biology of Violence: How Understanding the Brain, Behavior, and Environment Can Break the Vicious Circle of Aggression*. Free Press. 368 pages.

[25] Bremner, p. 797-805.

[26] van Praag, Henriette, Gerd Kempermann, & Fred H. Gage. 1999. Running increases cell proliferation and neurogenesis in the adult mouse dentate gyrus. In: *Nature Neuroscience*, vol. 2#3, March 1999. p.266-270.

Chapter 4: The Masterful Heart

[1] Flavia 1999. *Seeing*. Novato, CA: Portal Publications, Ltd.

[2] McCraty, Rollin & Institute of HeartMath. 1997. HeartMath Research Center. "Research Overview, Exploring the role of the heart in human performance." p. 3. HeartMath Research Center, 14700 West Park Ave., P.O. Box 1463, Boulder Creek, CA 95006. (831)338-8500 www.Heartmath.org

[3] Russek, L. B. and G. E. Schwartz. 1994 "Interpersonal Heart-Brain Registration and the Perception of Parental Love: A 42 Year Follow-up of the Harvard Mastery of Stress Study." *Subtle Energies*, 5, 3: pp. 195-208.

[4] Moss, T. 1979. *The Body Electric*. Jeremy P. Tarcher. Los Angeles, CA. p. 219.

[5] Pearce, Joseph Chilton. 1992. *Evolution's End, Claiming the Potential of our Intelligence*. Harper & Row, San Francisco, CA. p. 104.

[6] Pearsall, Paul. 1998. *The Heart's Code*. Broadway Books, NY. p. 78.

[7] Tortora, Gerard J. & Nicholas P. Anagnostakos. 1990. *The Principles Of Anatomy And Physiology (6TH ED.)* Harper & Row, NY. pp.590-591.

[8] Russek, L. B. and G. E. Schwartz. 1996. Energy cardiology: a dynamical energy systems approach for integrating conventional and alternative medicine. In: *Advances*, 12,(4): pp. 4-24.

[9] Russek, L. G. & G. E. Schwartz. 1996. pp. 4 – 24.

[10] Coulter, Dee Joy. 1986 *Enter the Child's World*. Coulter Pub., Longmont, CO. Sound cassette.

[11] Russek and Schwartz, 1996. pp. 4–24.

[12] Ragan, P. A., W. Wang & S. R. Eisenberg. 1995. Magnetically Induced Currents in the Canine Heart: A Finite Element Study. *IEEE Transactions in Biomedical Engineering*, vol. 42, pp. 110-115.

[13] Tiller, William. 1997. Science And Human Transformation; Subtle Energies, Intentionality and Consciousness. Pavior Pub., Walnut Creek, CA. p. 46.

[14] Capra, Fritjof. 2000. *The Tao of Physics; an exploration of the parallels between modern physics and Eastern mysticism*. Shambhala Press, Boston, MA.

[15] Russell, Peter. 1999. Science and Consciousness Conference, Albuquerque, N.M., April, 1999.

[16] Rivlin, Robert and Karen Gravelle. 1984. *Deciphering The Senses: The Expanding World of Human Perception*. Simon & Schuster, NY. p. 11.

[17] Ibid

[18] Ibid.

[19] Tiller, William. p. 278

[20] McCraty, Rollin. 2000. Personal conversation with Rollin McCraty, Director of Research, Institute of Heartmath *

[21] Armour, J. A. & J. Ardell. (Eds) 1994. *Neurocardiology*. Oxford U. Press, NY.

[22] Goleman, Daniel. 1995. *Emotional Intelligence*. Bantam Books, NY.

[23] Armour. J. A. 1991. Anatomy and function of the intrathoracic neurons regulating the mammalian heart. In: I H Zucker and J. P. Gilmore (eds.). *Reflex Control Of The Circulation*. Boca Raton, FL: CRC Press. pp.1-37.

[24] Pert, Candice B. 1997. *Molecules of Emotion*. Scribner, NY.

[25] Cantin, M. & J. Genest. 1986. The Heart as an Endocrine Gland. *Scientific American*, vol. 254, p. 76.

[26] Armour J. A. and J. Ardell (EDS). 1994. *Neurocardiology*. Oxford University Press, NY.

[27] Armour, J. A. 1991. pp. 1-37.

[28] McCraty, Rollin. 1997. p. 3.

[29] Rodriquez, Eugenio, et. al. 1999. Perception's shadow: long-distance syynchronization of human brain activity. *Nature*, Vol. 397, February4, 1999. pp. 430-433.

[30] McCraty, Rollin, William A. Tiller, and Mike Atkinson. 1995. Head-heart Entrainment: A Preliminary Survey. In: *Integrating the Science and Art of Energy Medicine: ISSSEEM Fifth Annual Conference Long Program and Proceedings*. ISSSEEM, Boulder, CO. pp. 26-30.

[31] McCraty, Rollin—new research, not yet published on alpha brain rhythm synchronization assisting cognitive learning following the HeartMath Institute's Cut-Through technique that brings the heart into coherence. Phone conversation, February, 2000.

[32] Lacey, John I. & Beatrice C. Lacey. 1978. Two-way communication between the heart and the brain: Significance of time within the cardiac cycle. *American Psychologist*. Feb. 1978. pp. 99-113.

[33] Jahn, R. G. and B. J. Dunne. 1997. Science of the Subjective, Technical Notes, Princeton University, New Jersey, March 1997. Research done at the Princeton Engineering Anomalies Research program at Princeton University. (P.E.A.R)

[34] Pearsall, Paul.

[35] Dunne, B. J. and R. G. Jahn. 1995. *Consciousness and Anomalous Physical Phenomenon Technical Notes*. Princeton University Press, Princeton, NJ.

[36] Dossey, Larry. 1993. *Healing Words: The Power of Prayer and the Practice of Medicine*. Harper Collins, NY.

[37] Czikszentmihalyi, Mihalyi. 1996. *Creativity; Flow and the Psychology of Discovery and Invention*. Harper Collins, NY. pp. 57-123, 259.

[38] Cheeah and Faroh, Adapted from the Yum Solution developed by Cheeah and Faroh. 1998.

Chapter 5: In the Beginning - Stress in Utero

[1] Diamond, Mariam. 1998. *Magic Trees of the Mind*. Dutton, NY. p.66.

[2] Alesandra Piontelli. 1987. Infant observation from before birth. *International Review of Psycho-analysis*. 16:413-426.

[3] Ludwig, Janus & Jason Aronson. 1997. The Enduring Effects of Prenatal Experience. Echos From the Womb. Ludwig Janus-Jason Aronson, Inc., NJ. pp. 6-12.

[4] Foresti, G. 1982. Mutterliche Angst und Zustande Kindlicker Ubererregbrakeit. In: Pranatale und Perinatale Psychosomatik. Ed. T. Han and S. Schindler, Stuttgart, Hippokrates.

[5] Bower, Thomas. 1984. The perceptual capacities of young children: The Magical World Television Series, July 16, 1984.

[6] William Condon & louis Sander. 1974. Neonate movement is synchronized with adult speech: Interactional participation and language acquisition. *Science.* Jan. 11:99-101.

[7] Ridgeway, Roy. 1987. The Unborn Child, How to recognize and overcome pre-natal trauma. London: Aldershot, Wildwood House. p.39.

[8] Gallia, Katherine, et. al. 1999. *Natural Health.* May 1999.

[9] Erich Bleschschmidt. 1977. *The Beginning of Human Life.* Springer-Verlag, NY.

[10] Goddard, Sally. 1996. *A Teachers Window To the Child's Mind*, and papers from the institute of neuro-physiological psychology. Fern Ridge Press, Eugene, OR. p. 7.

[11] Sontag, Lester W. 1966. War and the Maternal Fetal Relationship. Paper at the New York Academy of Science.

[12] Ridgeway, Roy. 1977. Sylvia Brody & S. Axelrod. p. 38

[13] Goddard, Sally. 1996 p. 7.

[14] Reinisch, et. al. 1978. Prenatal pregnasone exposure in humans and animals retards intrauterine growth. *Science*, 202, 436-438.

[15] Valman, H.B. & J. F Pearson, 1980. What the Fetus Feels. *British Med. J.* January 26, 1980.

[16] Ridgeway, Roy. 1977. Emil Reinhold, p. 5

[17] Sontag, Lester W. 1966.

[18] Rosenblith, J.F. 1990. Relations between Graham/Rosenblith neonatal measures and seven year assessments. Paper presented at International Conference on Infant Studies, Montreal.

[19] Nordberg, L. et al. 1989. Psychomotor and mental development during infancy: Relations to psychosocial conditions and health: Longitudinal study of children in a new Stockholm suburb. *Acta Paediatrica Scandinavica.* (Suppl. 353), 3 – 35.

[20] Frida, E. & M. Weinstock. 1988. Prenatal stress increases anxiety relationed behavior and alters cerebral lateralization of dopamine activity. *Life Science*, 42:1059-1065.

[21] Theodor Hau. 1982. Narzi Bmus und Internationitat pra – und perinatale Aspekte. In: *Pranatale und Perinatale Psychosomatik*, ed. T. Hau & S. Schindler. Stuttgart, Hippokrates

[22] Ridgeway, Roy. p. 5.

[23] Liley, A.M. 1977. The Foetus as a personality. Self and Society, June, 1977.

[24] Field, T. 1998. Maternal depression effects on infants and early interventions. In: *Preventative Medicine*, 27:200-203.

[25] Ashley Montague. 1964. *Life Before Birth.* New American Library, NY. Experiment with D.K. Spelt.

[26] Verny, Thomas and John Kelly. 1982. *The Secret Life Of The Unborn Child.* Collins, Toronto. TUC, p. 18

[27] DeCasper, Anthony and William P. Fifer. 1984. Study TUC, RIDG. .36

[28] Ridgeway, Roy. 1973. Dominick Purpura, ed. *Am. J. Brain Research*. p. 26

[29] Verney, T. and John Kelly.

[30] Gerhard Rottman. 1974. Unterscuchungen uber die Einstellung zur Schwangerschaft und zur Fotolens Entwickling. In Prenatale Psychologie. Ed. G.H. Grober, Munich, Kindler

[31] Gerhard Amendt & Michael Schwartz. 1992. *Das Leben unerwunschter kinder*. Frankfurt/Main: Fischer.

[32] Bergh, B. 1990. The influence of maternal emotions during pregnancy on fetal and neonatal behavior. In: Pre- and Parinatal Psychology. 5:119-130.

[33] B. Zuckerman, H. Amaro, et. al. 1989. Depresssive symptoms during pregnancy: Relationship to poor health behaviors. *Am. J. of Obstetrics & Gynecology*, 160:1107-1111.

[34] Coulter, Dr. Dee Joy. 1993. *Movement, Meaning and the Mind*. Keynote Address, Seventh Annual Educational Kinesiology Foundation Gathering, Greeley, Colorado. July. 1993.

[35] Lee, K. Y. C, Jurgen Klinger, & Harden McConnell. 1994. Electric field-induced concentration gradients in lipid monolayers. In: *Science*, Feb. 4, 1994, (vol. 263), pp. 655-658.

[36] Ongur, Dost. 1999. Depression: Beyond Seratonin. *Psychology Today*, March/April, 1999. p.72 From talk at 1999 Society of Neuroscience.

[37] McEwen, Bruce. Director of neurobiology lab at New York's Rockefeller University. Ibid. pp. 36 & 72. Watanabe, Y., Stone. E., & McEwen. B.X. 1994. Induction and habituation of c-fos and zif/268 by acute and repeated stressors. *Neuroreport*. 5:1321-1324.

[38] Duman, Ronald. 1999. Depression: Beyond Seratonin. *Psychology Today*, March/April 1999. p. 35.

[39] Veldman, Frans. 1994. Confirming affectivity in the dawn of life. *International J. of Prenatal and Perinatal Psychology and Medicine*. 6:11-26.

[40] Hatch, Maureen, et. al. 1993. *American Journal of Epidemiology*. May 15, 1993 In: *Science News*, vol. 144, p. 36, July 17, 1993.

[41] Beauchamp, Gary K. & Richard H. Porter. 1995. *Proceedings of the National Academy of Sciences*. March 28, 1995.

[42] Pert, Candace B. 1997. *Molecules of Emotion*. New York: Scribner.

[43] Pearce, Joseph Chilton. 1992. *Evolutions End*, p. 113-114.

[44] Levine, Seymour. 1960. Stimulation in Infancy. *Scientific American*, May 1960. pp. 80-86.

[45] Isaacs, Charles E. 1995. Ways Mother's Milk Fights Disease. Experimental Biology Conference in Atlanta, Georgia.

[46] Odent, Michael. 1997. The Scientification of Love. Presented at the Society for Effective Affective Learning, 7th International Conference, April 3-6, The University of Bath, England.

[47] Prescott, James. 1997. Intelligence of Play Video. Touch the Future. Nevada City, California.

[48] Tortora, Gerard J. & Nicholas P. Anagnostakos. 1990. PRINCIPLES OF ANATOMY AND PHYSIOLOGY (6th Ed.). Harper & Row, N.Y. p. 409.

[49] Pearce, Joseph Chilton. 1992. p. 122-123.

[50] Baily, Jean, 1999. Coordinator of child and adolescent mental-health services at Lutheran Medical Center in Brooklyn, N.Y. IN, *Time Magazine*, July 5, 1999. p. 58.

[51] Odent, Michael. 1997. p. 23.

[52] Huxley, Laura Archera. 1992. THE CHILD OF YOUR DREAMS. Destiny Books, One Park Street, Rochester, VT, 05767.

Chapter 6: The Shapes of Our Reality

[1] Chopra, Deepak. 1998. *Consciousness Conference in Denver*, Colorado. July, 1998.

[2] Russell, Peter, 1999. *The Consciousness Revolution*, A Transatlantic Dialogue with Stan Grof and Ervin Laszlo. London: Element Books.
 Russell, Peter, 2000. *From Science to God, A Physicist's Exploration of the Light of Consciousness*. England: Elf Rick Pub.

[3] Zion, Leela C. 1986 The Physical Side of Thinking. Making Sense: Kinesthesia. C.C. Thomas, Springfield, Ill. Also: Zion, L. 1994. 'The Physical Side of Learning: A parent-teacher's guidebook of physical activities kids need to be successful in school. Front Row Experience, Byron, CA.

[4] Lakoff, George and Mark Johnson. 1999. *Philosophy in the Flesh*. Basic Books, NY.

[5] Hainline, Louise. 1998. The development of basic visual abilities. In: *Perceptual Development, Visual, Auditory and Speech Perception in Infancy*. Ed. Alan Slater. East Sussex, UK: Psychology Press. pp. 5-42.

[6] Wilson, Frank R. 1998. *The Hand; How It's Use Shapes the Brain, Language, and Human Culture*. Pantheon Books, NY. Introduction.

[7] Cohen, Mark S. 1996. Visual Perception. *Brain Journal*, Feb. 27, 1996. Science News, Vol. 149. p. 155, March 1, 1996.

[8] Sereno, et. al. 1995. Borders of multiple visual areas in humans revealed by functional MRI. *Science*, 268, 889-893.

[9] Russell, Peter, 1999. Science and Consciousness Conference.

[10] Rock, I. 1967. The Nature Of Perceptual Adaptation. Basic Books., NY.

[11] Sibatani, Atuhiro. 1980. The Japanese Brain, The difference between East and West may be the different between left and right. *Science*, 80, December. pp. 22-27.

[12] Hebb, D.O. 1949. *The Organization of Behavior*. John Wiley and Sons, NY. p. 289-294.

[13] Tiller, William A. 1997. *Science Of Human Transformation; Subtle Energies, Intentionality and Consciousness*. Pavior Pub., Walnut Creek, CA. p. 148.

[14] Gopnik, Alison, Andrew N. Meltzoff, and Particia Kuhl. 1999. *The Scientist In The Crib*. William Morrow and Company, Inc., NY.

[15] Prigogine, Ilya and Isabelle Stengers. 1984. *Order Out of Chaos: Man's New Dialogue with Nature*. Random House, NY.

[16] Recanzone and Merzenich, Michael Kilgard, Learning Brain Expo 2001,

Austin, TX, July 2001.

[17] Pribrim, Karl. 1982. Karl Pribrim interview with Judith Hopper. *Omni*, October 1982. p. 72.

[18] Dossey, Larry. 1994. Larry Dossey in Conversation with Michael Toms. Audio-tape. Aslan Pub., Lower Lake, CA.

[19] Tiller, William. p. 70-75.

[20] Ibid. p. 63.

[21] Aspect, A. , J. Dalibard, and G. Rogen. 1982. The EPR Paradox. *Physics Review Letter*, Vol. 49, p. 1804.

[22] Goswani, Amit. 1999. Quantum Physics, Consciousness, Creativity.... Science of Consciousness Conference, Albuquerqe, N.M. April, 1999.

[23] Shearer, A. 1989. *Effortless Being*. London: Mandala University Paperbacks. p. 9

[24] Maharishi University Studies and studies discussed by Larry Dossey.

[25] Radin, Dean. 1997. *The Conscous Universe: The Scientific Truth of Psychic Phenomena*. Harper Edge.

[26] Mander, Jerry. 1978. *Four Arguments For The Elimination Of Television*. Quill Pub., NY.

[27] Pearce, Joseph Chilton. 1999. Educational Kinesiology Gathering, Vancouver, B.C., July, 1999.

[28] Mander, Jerry. 1978.

[29] Orme-Johnson, David. 1988. *Journal of Conflict Resolution*. Ann-Arbor, MI, Department of Journalism, U. of Michigan. In: *Science News*.

[30] Tiller, William A., Walter E. Dibble, Jr., and Michael J. Kohane. 1999. Exploring Robust Interactions between Human Intention and Inanimate/ Animate Systems. Presented at Toward a Science of Consciousness – Fundamental Approaches. May 25 – 28, 1999. Tokyo, Japan: United Nations University. Information available through Ditron, LLC, P.O. Box 70, Excelsior, MN. 55331, USA.

[31] Rubic, Beverley. 1999. Subtle Information: A Unifing Concept for Matter and Consciousness. Toward a Science of Consciousness Conference, Albuquerque, N.M. April.

[32] Tiller, William A., Walter E. Dibble, and Michael J. Kohane. 2001. *Conscious Acts of Creation, The Emergence of a New Physics*. Pavior Publishing, Walnut Creek, CA. (www.pavior.com)

[33] Pearce, Joseph Chilton. 1999. Science and Consciousness Conference, Albuquerque, NM. April, 1999.

[34] Tiller, William. 1997.

[35] Sousa, David A. 1995. *How the Brain Learns*. Reston, VA: The National Association of Secondary School Principals. p. 10.

[36] Sylwester, Robert. 1995 *A Celebration of Neurons*. ASCD Publication. Chapter 4.

[37] Schwartz, G. E. & L. G. Russek. 1996. Do All Dynamic Systems Have Memory? Implications of the Systemic Memory Hypothesis for Science & Society, In: *Brain And Values: Behavioral Neurodynamics* v. Ed. K. Hl.Y. Pribram

& J. S. King. Lawrence Erlbaum Assoc., NY.
[38] Pearsall, Paul. 1998. *The Hearts Code*. Broadway Books, NY.
[39] Lashley, K. S. 1950. In Search of the Engram. Symposia of the Society for Experimental Biology. 4, P. 478.
[40] Pribrum, Karl. 1982. Karl Pribrum Interview with Judith Hooper. *Omni Magazine*. October 1982.
[41] Gerber, Richard. 1988. *Vibrational Medicine*. Bear & Co., Santa Fe, NM. pp. 45-48.
[42] Pribrium, Karl. 1971. *Languages of the Brain*. Englewood Cliff: Prentice Hall.
[43] Pribrum, Karl H. 1991. *Brain and Perception; Holonomy and Structue in Figural Processing*. Lawrence Erlbaum Assoc., NY.
Pribrium, Karl H. 1994. *Origins: Brain and Self Organization*. Lawrence Erlbaum Assoc., NY.
[44] Pert, Candice. 1999. *Molecules of Emotion, Why You Feel the Way You Feel*. Simon & Schuster, NY. pp. 135-148.
[45] Ibid.
[46] Ibid.
[47] Stokes, Gordon and Daniel Whiteside. 1985. *Tools of the Trade*. Applied Kinesiology Press, Tucson, AZ.
[48] Pert, Candace. p. 148.
[49] Jung, Carl. 1978. *Collected Works*. Princeton University Press, Princeton, NJ.
[50] Sheldrake, Rupert. 1995. *The Hypothesis of A New Science of Life, Morphic Resonance*. Park Street Press, Rochester, VT. p. 13.
[51] Roush, Wade. 1995. Defining the first steps on the path toward cell specialization. In: *Science*, vol. 270. October 27. pp.578-579.
[52] Tortora, Gerard J. and Nicholas P. Anagnostakos. 1990. *Principles of Anatomy And Physiology. 6th ed.* Harper and Row, NY. p. 933.
[53] Burr, Harold S. 1972. *The Fields of Life*. Ballantine Books, NY.
[54] Kirlian, Semyon and V. Kirlian. 1961. Photography and Visual Observations by Means of High Frequency Currents. *Journal of Scientific and Applied Photography*. Vol. 6, pp. 145-148.
[55] Gerber, Richard.
[56] Gerber, Richard. pp.51, 60, 111-112.
[57] Gerber, Richard. p. 60.
[58] Tiller, William. 1997. pp. 172-175.
[59] Satir, Virginia. 1984 *Becoming Whole*. New Dimensions Radio 6/14/84, #1881.
[60] Ingber, Donald E. 1998. The Architecture of Life. *Scientific American*, January 1998. pp. 48-57.

Chapter 7: Sound - the Cosmic Motor

[1] Truax, Barry. Communication Professor, Fraser University, Burnaby, British Columbia.
[2] Nijhuis, J. G. 1992. (Ed.) Fetal behavior—developmental and perinatal aspects. In: *Niuhuis*, Oxford U. Press. p. 133.

[3] Bernard, J, and Sontag, L. 1947. Fetal reactions to sound. *Journal of Genetic Psychology*. 70:209-10.

[4] Yogananda, Paramahansa. 1990. *Scientific Healing Affirmations*. Self-Realization Fellowship. Ninth Ed.

[5] Elinasto, Jaan. 1997. A 120-Mpc perodicity in the three-dimensional distribution of galaxy superclusters. *Nature*, 385:139-141.

[6] Szalay, Alexander, S. 1996. *Texas Symposium of Relativistic Astrophysics*, Chicago, Dec. 1996. Baltimore.MD. John Hopkins U.

[7] Jenny, Hans. 1974. *Cymatics*. AG,Switzerland: Basilius Presse.

[8] Halpern. 1985. *Sound Health, The Music and Sounds that Make us Whole*. Harper & Row, San Francisco, CA. pp. 33-39.

[9] Braden, Gregg. 1997. *Awakening To Zero Point. The collective Initiation*. Belleview, WA: Radio Bookstore Press. pp. 70-71.

[10] Emoto, Masaru. 2001. *Messages from Water*, World's First Pictures of Frozen Water Crystals. I.H.M. General Research Institute, HADO Kyoikusha Co., Ltd.

[11] Halpern, Steven. 1985. pp. 32-36.

[12] Manners, Peter. 1980. The Future of Cymatic Therapy. In: *Technology Tomorrow*, June, 1980.

[13] Manners, Peter Guy, 1976, *Cymatics Therapy; Sound and Vibratory Pattern Research*. Bretforton, England.

[14] Ingber, Donald E. 1998. The architecture of life. *Scientific American*, Jan. 1998. pp. 48-57.

[15] Campbell, Don. 2000. *Mozart Effect for Children*. Morrow, NY.

[16] Braden, Gregg. 1997. pp. 28-29.

[17] Halpern, Steven1985. *Sound Health, The Music and Sounds That Make Us Whole*. Harper & Row. San Francisco, CA. p. 38.

[18] Braden, Gregg. 1997. pp. 28-31.

[19] Schafer, R. Murray. *The Tuning of the World*. Knopf, NY. 1977.

[20] Mendelsohn, Robert S., M.D. 1979. *Confessions of A Medical Heretic*. Warner Books, NY.

[21] Swicord, Mays. 1984. Biophysicist with the National Center for Devices and Radio-Logical Health at the (FDA). In; *Science News*, April 24, 1984.

[22] Brewer, Chris and Don Campbell. 1991. *Rhythms of Learning*. Zephyr Press, Tuscon, Az. p. 20

[23] Ibid.

[24] Goddard, Sally. 1996. *A Teacher's Window into the Child's Mind*. Eugene, OR: Fern Ridge Press. p. 44 and Steinbach, 1994.

[25] Papansek, Hanus. Musicality in infancy research; biological and cultural origins of early musicality. In: *Musical Beginnings*, Irene Deliege and John Slovoa (EDS), Oxford University Press. pp. 37-51.

[26] Effects of intense noise during fetal life upon postnatal adaptability. *J. of Acoustical Soc. of America*. 47, 1128-1130, 1970.

[27] The Committee on Hearing, Bioacoustics & Biomechanics of the National Research Council, 1982. Prenatal effects of exposure to high-level noise.

Washington, DC: National Academic Press.

[28] Ibid.

[29] Campbell, Don. 2000. *The Mozart Effect for Children*. New York: William Morrow Pub. p. 54.

[30] Ayers, A. Jean. *Sensory Integration and Learning Disorders*. Western Psychological Services, Los Angeles, CA. p. 70.

[31] Hernandez-Peon, R. 1969. Neurophysiology of Attention. In: J. J Vinkin & G. W. Bruyun(eds.) *Handbook of Clinical Neurology.* North Holland Pub., Amsterdam.

[32] Pearce, Joseph Chilton. 1974. *The Magical Child* . Brody, Sylvia & S. Axelrod. Dutton, Pub., NY.

[33] LeCanuet. J.P. et. al. 1988. Fetal cardiac, and motor responses to octive-band noises as a function of cerebral frequency, intensity and heart rate variability. *Early Human Development*, 18:81-93.

[34] Condon, William F. 1999. *New Dimensions Synthesis of Great Interviews*. New Dimensions Radio, San Francisco, CA.

[35] Condon, William F. and Louis Sander 1974. Boston U. RRp. 38
6 1973. Statistical studies on the effects of intense noise during fetal life. *J. of Sound Vibrations*, 27, 101-111. Also, F.N. Jones & Tauscher, J. 1978. Residence under an airport landing pattern as a factor in autism. *Archives of Environmental Health*, 35, 10-12.

[36] Pearce, Joseph Chilton. 1974. p. 71.

[37] Tomatis, Alfred A. 1997. *The Ear and Language*. Stoddart Pub.
1992. *The Conscious Ear – My Life of Transformation through Listening*. Talman, Co. Pub.

[38] Goddard, Sally.

[39] Ridgeway, Roy. 1987. *The Unborn Child, How to Recognize and Overcome Prenatal trauma*. Wildwood House, Ltd., London, England. p. 20.

[40] Ibid. p. 17.

[41] Liley, A.M. The Foetus as a Personality. *Self and Society*, June, 1977.

[42] Tiller, William, Rollin McCraty, Mike Atkinson. 1996. Cardiac Coherence: A new, noninvasive measure of autonomic nervous system order. *Alternative Therapies*, January 1996, Vol. 2(1):52.

[43] Odent, Michelle. 1986. *Primal Health, A Blueprint for Our Survival*. Century, Hutchinson, Ltd. p. 30.

[44] Rodriquez, Eugenio. et al. 1999. Perceptions Shadow; long-distance synchronization of human brain activity. *Nature*, Vol. 397. February4, 1999. pp. 430-433.

[45] Redmond, Layne. 1999. Primal Sound: The Beat of the Drum. *New Dimensions*, July-August. 1999. p. 20.

[46] Schwartz, Peter John, et. al. 1998. Infant Deaths Linked to Odd Heartbeat. *New England Journal of Medicine*. June 11, 1998.

[47] Prescott, James. 1997. *Discovering The Intelligence of Play*. Video. Touch The Future Foundation.

[48] Weikert, Phyllis S. 2000. Personal correspondence during a course in Michigan, April, 2000.

[49] Weikert, Phyllis S. Ibid.

[50] Weikert, Phyllis S., & Elizabeth B. Carlton. 1995. *Foundations In Elementary Education: Movement*. High/Scope Press, Ypsilanti, Michigan.

[51] Cockerton, T, Moore, S. and Norman, D. 1997. Cognitive test performance and background music. In: *Perceptual and Motor Skills*. 85:1435-1438.

[52] Hughes, J. R., Daaboul,Y., Fino, J.J. & Shaw, Gordon. 1998. The Mozart effect on epileptiform activity. In: *Clinical Electroencephalography*, 29:109-119.

[53] Parsons, L.M.; M.J. Martinez; E.D. Delosh; A. Halpern; and M.H. Thaut. 2001. Musical and Visual Priming of Visualization and Mental Rotation. IN PROCESS.

[54] Szmedra. L. & D. W. Bacharach. 1998. Effect of music on perceived exertion, plasma lactate, norepinephrine, and cardiovascular hemodynamics during treadmill running. In: *International Journal of Sports Medicine*. 19:32-37.

[55] The Yellow Emperior's Classic of Internal Medicine, Simple Questions (Huang Ti Nei Jing Su Wen) 1979. People's Health Pub. House, Beijing. P. 28. First Published C. 100 BC.

[56] Campbell, Don. 2000.

[57] Hodges, Donald. 2000. Implications of Music and Brain Research. *Music Educators Journal* Special Focus Issue: Music and the Brain, 87:2, 17-22.

[58] Weinberger, N.M. 1994. The Musical Infant. MUSICA Research Newsletter, Spring 1994.

[59] Balaban, M.T., L. M. Anderson & A. B. Wisniewski. 1998. Lateral asymmetries in infant melody perception. In: *Developmental Psychology*, 34-48.

[60] Burns, M. T. 1988. Music as a tool for enhancing creativity. *Journal of Creative Behavior*, 22:62-69.

[61] Wiggins, J. H. 1994. Children's strategies for solving compositional problems with peers. *Journal of Research in Music Education*, 42:232-252.

[62] Kratus, J. 1994. Relationships among children's music audition and their compositional processes and products. *J. of Research in Music Education*, 42:115-130.

[63] Jourdain, Robert. 1997. *Music, the Brain and Ecstasy*. Avon Books, Inc. NY. p. 4.

[64] The College Board, 1992 Profile of SAT and Achievement Test Takers, College Entrance Examination Board, p. 3.

[65] Cutietta, Robert, et al. 2000. Spin-offs, The Extra-Musical Advantages of a Musical Education. United Instruments, Inc. Future of Music Project.

[66] Goddard, Sally. 1996 p. 55

[67] Beaulieu, John. 1987. *Sound in the Healing Arts*. Station Hill Publishers, London.

[68] Schlaug, Gottfried, and Gaser Christian. 2001. Musical Training During Childhood May Influence Regional Brain Growth. Paper presented at the 53rd Annual Meeting of the American Academy of Neurology, Philadelphia, PA. May 16, 2001.

[69] Pantev, C, et. al. 1998. Increased cortical representation in musicians. Scientific Correspondence. In *Nature*. 396(128):811-813.

[70] Hodges, Donald. 1996. Neuromusical Research: A Review of the Literature. In: *Handbook of Music Psychology*, 2nd ed. Ed. D. Hodges, 203-290.

[71] Hodges, Donald. 2000. pp., 17-22.

[72] Kindermusik: P.O. Box 26575, Greensborough, North Carolina 27415 Phone: 1-800-628-5687Website: www.kindermusik.com
Musikgarten: 409 Blandwood Ave., Greensborough, North Carolina 27401 Phone: 1-800-216-6864.
Music With Mar: 149 Garland Circle, Palm Harbor, Fl. 34683. Phone (727)545-4627Website: www.musicwithmar.com

[73] Johnson, Michael. Musician and teacher in Salt Lake City, Utah. Personal conversation.

[74] Nichols, Michael. 1996. *The Lost Art of Listening*. Ingram Books, Guilford Pub., Tennesee.

[75] Tomatis, Lena A. 1978. The multi-disciplinary aspects of audio-psycho-phonology. Paper presented at the 5th International Congress of Audio-Psycho-Phonology, Toronto, May, 1978.

[76] Ladinsky, Daniel. 1999. *The Gift*, Poems by HAFIZ, The Great Sufi Master. Penguin/Arkana Pub., NY, NY. P. 99.

Chapter 8: Language - Sound in Motion

[1] Jourdain, Robert. 1997. *Music, the Brain and Ecstasy*. Avon Books, Inc. NY. p. 275.

[2] Berard, Guy. 1993. *Hearing Equals Behavior*. Keats Pub., Inc. New Canaan, CT., pp. 15-37.

[3] McDermott, Jeanne. 1983. The Solid-State Parrot. Science 83', pp. 59-65.

[4] Goddard, Sally. pp. 54-55.

[5] Halpern, Steven. p. 32.

[6] Taggart, Cynthia Crump. 1998. The effect of instruction on the music potential of young children. Suzuki Assoc. of America Conference.

[7] *Time Magazine*, February 14, 2000, Number Section, p. 25.

[8] Healy, Jane M. 1990. *Endangered Minds, Why Children Don't Think and What we Can Do About It*. Simon & Schuster, NY. pp. 86-104.

[9] Campbell, Don. 2000.

[10] White, David.1999. Science and Spirituality, Summer Conference, Denver, Colorado. July, 1999.

[11] Berard, Guy. p. 4.

[12] Fjordbo, Gitte Dollerup. 1995. Why We Have To Crawl ...or on the Development of Human Motor and Communicative Skills – Aberrations and Inter-connections. MA. Thesis, University of Copenhagen, Denmark p. 169-170.

[13] Ayers, Jean. 1982. *Sensory Integration and the Child*. Western Psychological Services, Los Angeles, CA.

[14] Berard, Guy. p. 15-37.

[15] Goddard, Sally,p. 24

[16] Galaburda, Albert M. 1994. Evidence for abberant auditory anatomy in developmental dyslexia. In: Proceedings of the National Academy of Science. Vol. 91, pp. 8010-8013. Aug. 1994.

[17] Goddard, Sally. pp. 16 – 18.

[18] Ibid. p. 43.

[19] Fjordbro, Gette D. 1995.

[20] Talal M. Nsouli, et. al. 1994. *Annals of Allergy*, Sept. 1994.

[21] Brooks, Adrienne C. 1994. Middle ear infections in children. *Science News*, vol 146, November 9, 1994, p. 332

[22] Levinson, Frank J. & Harold N. 1973. Dysmetric Dyslexia and Dyspraxia: Hypothesis and Study. In: *Journal of American Academy of Child Psychiatry*. Vol. 12, pp. 690-701.

[23] Levinson, Harold N. 1992. *Turning Around the Upside-Down Kids,, Helping Dyslexic Kids Overcome Their Disorder*. M. Evans. NY.

[24] Goddard, Sally p. 50, also A. Tomatis.

[25] Fjordbo, Gitte Dollerup. 1995. Why We Have To Crawl... On the development of human motor and communicative skills, aberrations and interconnections. Copenhagen, MA. Thesis on Audiologopedics.

[26]Johansen, Kjeld. 1995. Frequency specific left hemisphere stimulation with music and sounds in dyslexia remediation. 3rd European Music Therapy Conference, 17-20 June,, 1995, Aalborg, Denmark. Kjeld Johansen, Director of Research, Baltic Dyslexia Research Lab, Ro Skolevej 14, DK-3760 Gudhjem, Bornholm, Denmark. EMAIL: paedacon@dk-online.dk

[27] Nagarajan, Srikantan & Michael M. Merzenich.1999. Sound and Dyslexia. Proceedings of the National Academy of Sciences, May 25, 1999.

[28] Berard, Guy.

[29] Tallal, Paula, et. al. 1993. Neurobiological basis of speech: a case for the Pre-eminence of temporal processing. In: Tallal, Galaburda and Euler (eds.); Temporal Processing in the Nervous System. The New York Academy of Sciences, NY.

[30] Campbell, Don. 2000

[31] Crandell, Carl. 1998. "Classroom Acoustics; A failing Grade", Hearing Health, Sept/Oct. 1998 pp. 11 –59.

[32] Berard, Guy.

[33] Halpern, Steven. p. 82. A. Tomatis

[34] Livingston, Richard. 1993. Journal of the American Academy of Child and Adolescent Psychiatry,May, 1993. In: *Science News*, May 1, 1993, vol. 143, p. 278.

[35] Diamond, Marion C. 1991. Hormonal Effects on the Development of Cerebral Lateralization. Psychoneuroendocrinology. 16:121-129.

[36] Paulesu, Eraldo and Elise Temple. 2001. Dyslexia. University of Milan, Biocca, Italy and Stanford University. *Science*, March 16, 2001

[37] Fjordbro, Gitte D. 1995.

[38] Johansen, Kjeld. 1995

[39] Johansen, Kjeld. 1991. Diagnosing Dyslexia: The Screening of Auditory Laterality. AND Some Thoughts on Research In Dyslexia and Related Disorders. Available from ERIC, order no. ED 326 845.

[40] Berard, Guy. p. 15-37.

[41] Goddard, Sally. 1996. p. 48-60.

[42] Johansen, Kjeld. 1995

[43] Goddard, Sally. p. 55

Chapter 9: Play - Opener of the Heart

[1] Brown, Stuart L. 1995. Through the Lens of Play. In: *Revision* vol. 17(4):4-12.

[2] Teitel, Jay. 1999. The Kidnapping of Play. In: *Saturday Night*, April 1999. p 57.

[3] Brown, Stuart L. 1999. Play, Learning Without Limits, Exploring the Intelligence of Play. Touch The Future Conference, Monterey, Calif, January 1999.

[4] Meeker, Joseph W. 1995. Comedy and a Play Ethic. In: *ReVision*, vol 17, No. 4.

[5] Meeker, Joseph. 1997. The Comedy of Survival; Literacy Ecology and a Play Ethic. University of Arizona Press, Tucson, AZ.

[6] Brown, Stewart L. 1994. Animals at play. *National Geographic*. 186(6):2-35.

[7] Panksepp, Jaak. 1998. *Affective Neuroscience, The Foundations of Human and animal Emotions*. Oxford University Press. p. 281-282.

[8] Panksepp. p. 291.

[9] Panksepp. p. 281.

[10] Panksepp. pp. 280-281

[11] Siviy, Stephen. 1998. Play. Psycholgiologist at Gettysburg College, PA.

[12] Montague, Ashley. 1989. *Growing Young.*, Bergin & Garvey, NY. 292 p.

[13] Goddard, Sally. 1996. *A Teacher's Window Into The Child's Mind*. Fern Ridge Press, Eugene, Oregon. Pl. 40 –41.

[14] Roberts, Debra. 1997. ABC News 20/20, Brandy Binder Story. Documentary Editor, Debra Roberts. October 3, 1997

[15] Wennekes, Renate & Angelika Stiller. 1999. Developmental Kinesiology Intengration of our Senses. Institut fur kinesiologische Lernforderung, Neuenkirchen-Vorden, Germany. Course, July, 1999.

[16] Wennekes, Renate & Angelika Stiller, Story from Kukelhaus, Germany,

[17] Ibid.

[18] Ibid.

[19] Cohen, R. Irun. 1999. Institute of Science in Rehovot, Israel, In: *Science News*, 156, Aug. 14, 1999, pp 108.

[20] Carpenter, Siri. 1999. Modern Hygiene's Dirty Tricks, the clean life may throw off a delicate balance in the immune system. *Science News*, Vol. 156, Aug. 14, 1999. pp. 1088-110.

21 Sacks, David L & Shaden Kamhawi. 1999. Fly bites help guard against Leishmania. May 1999 meeting of the American Society of Microbiology in Chicago.

22 Eriksson, Peter S., Fred H. Gage, et. al. 1998. Neurogenesis in the Adult Human Hippocampus. In: *Nature Medicine*, 4(11),1313-1317, November

23 vanPragg, Henriette, et al. 1999. Running increases cell proliferation and neurogenesis in the adult mouse dentate gyrus. In: *Nature Neuroscience* 2(3)266-270. March

24 Gould, Elizabeth. et al. 1999. Learning enhances adult neurogenesis in the hippocampal formation. In: *Nature Neuroscience*, 2(3)260-265. March

25 Ayers, A Jean. 1982. *Sensory Integation and the Child*. Western Psychological Services, Los Angeles, CA.

26 Brown, Stuart L. 1995. p 6.

27 Teitelbaum, Philip. 1997. *Physiological Psychology: Fundamental Principals*. Englewood Cliffs, Prentice Hall, NJ.

28 Hannaford, Carla. 1995. *Smart Moves, Why Learning is Not All In Your Head*. pp. 117-119, 124-125.

29 White, Sally S. 1998. *Building A Labyrinth on a Shoestring Budget*. Physical Education Department, Palm Bay Elementary, 1200. Allamanda Rd., NE., Palm Bay. Fl. 32905. Also: The St. Louis Labyrinth Project, c/o Robert Ferre, 3124 Gurney Avenue, St. Louis, MO 63116. Phone (800)873-9873.

30 Pyfer, J., Johnson R. 1981. Factors affecting motor delays. Excerpts from adapted physical activity. Eason, Smith & Caron, Human Kinetics Publishers, Box 5076, Champaign, Ill. 61820. Also, Crowe, Walter C., David Auxter & Jean Pyfer. 1981. Principles & methods of adapted physical education and recreation. C.V. Mosby Co., St. Louis, MO.

31 Sylwester, Robert. 1995. *A Celebration of Neurons: An Educator's Guide to the Human Brain*. Alexandria, VA. Association for Supervision and Curriculum Development. p. 158.

32 Goddard, p. 47.

33 Sylwester. 1995. p. 37.

34 Ackerman, Diane. 1990. *A Natural History of the Senses*. Vintage Books, NY. pp. 76-77.

35 Ibid, p. 77.

36 Wegschneider-Cruse, Sharon. 1997. *Family Reconstruction; The Living Theater Model*. Science and Behavior Books. The Family Trap.

37 Goddard, Sally, p. 45.

38 Maciocia, Giovanni. 1994. *The Practice of Chinese Medicine*. Churchill Livingston Pub., Edinburgh, London. p. 200.

39 McCraty, Rollin, Mike Atkinson, Dana Tomasino and William A. Tiller, 1998. The Electricity of Touch: detection and measurement of cardiac energy exchange between people. In: K. H. Pribram, ed. Brain and Values: Is a Biological Science of Values Possible. Mahwah, NY.: Lawrence Erlbaum Associates, Inc. p. 7.

40 Penksapp, p. 287-310.

[41] Penksapp. p. 289.

[42] Penksapp. pp. 287-290

[43] Penksapp. p. 33.

[44] Zajonc, Robert B. 1985. The Face of Emotion. Science, April 5, 1985, In: *Science News*, June 6, 1985, vol. 128.

[45] Penksapp. p. 280

[46] Provine, Albert. 2000. *Laughter, A Scientific Investigation*. Viking Penquine, NJ.

[47] Penksapp. p. 280.

[48] Brown, Stewart.1995. p. 11.

[49] Singer, Dorothy and Jerome. 1990. *The House Of Make Believe, Childrens Play and the Developing Imagination*. Harvard U. Press, Cambridge, MA.

[50] Penksapp. p. 280.

[51] Brown, Stewart. 1995. pp. 4-12.

[52] Singer, Dorothy and Jerome.

[53] Steven Sivey—and Singer.

[54] McLean, Paul D. 1990. *The Triune Brain In Evolution, Role in Paleocerebral Functions*. Plenum Press, NY. p. 559.

[55] Penksapp, p. 281.

[56] Pearce, Joseph Chilton. 1993. *Evolutions End*. pp. 160-162.

[57] Meeker, Joseph W. 1995. p. 23.

[58] Tietel, Jay. 1999. pp. 59-60.

[59] Prescott, James, Harry Harlow, Bill Mason & Chris Berkeson. At Hazelton Labs, Falls, Church, MI. Rock a Buy Baby – PBS Documentary.

[60] Prescott, James. 1979. Nurturing in Indigenous People. *Psychology Today*, December 1979.

[61] Prescott, James. 1997. Discovering the Intelligence of Play. Video. Touch The Future Foundation, Nevada City, CA.

[62] Perry, Bruce. 1998. Secrets to Academic Success. In: *Time Magazine*, Claudia Wallis article, October 19, 1998.

[63] Brown, Stewart. 1997. Discovering The Intelligence of Play. video

[64] Penksepp. pp. 283-17.

[65] White, Bowen. 1999. Why Normal Isn't Healthy. Touch the Future Conference, Monterey, CA. January 1999.

[66] Brown, Stewart. 1997.

[67] Brinson, Cynthia. 1999. Comment in *USA Today*, April 23, 1999. Doylestown, Pa.

[68] Prescott, James W. 1979.

[69] Hogan, Chuck. 1999. Staying in the Zone. Learning Without Limits, Exploring the Intelligence of Play. Touch the Future Conference, Jan. 1999.

[70] Hannaford, Carla. 1997. *The Dominance Factor, How Knowing Your Dominant Eye, Ear, Brain, Hand & Foot Can Improve Your Learning*. Great Ocean Pub., Arlington, VA. p. 127.

[71] Crum, Thomas. 1987. *The Magic of Conflict, Turning a Life of Work Into a Work of Art*. Simon & Schuster, NY.

[72] Donaldson, O. Fred. 1999. *Learning Without Limits*, Exploring the Intelligence of Play Conference, Jan. 1999 also Co-Creative Workshop together in Capt. Cook, Hawaii, March, 1999.

[73] Ayres, A. Jean. 1972. *Sensory Integration and Learning Disorders*. Western Psychological Services, Los Angeles. p. 58.

Chapter 10: How to Educate - the Wald Kindergarten

[1] Wald Kindergarten, Patrick Friedrich, Zartenerstr. 7, 79199 Kirchzarten, Germany. Phone: 07661/627272

[2] Ministry of Education and Research, International Relations Divison. Characteristic Features of Danish Education. Copenhagen, Denmark. 1992. p. 1-39.

[3] Skegler, Robert S. & Elzbeth Stern. 1998. Natural Learning. *Journal of Experimental Psychology*: General. December 1998.

[4] Kohn, Alfe. 1999. *The Schools Our Children Deserve: Moving Beyond Traditional Classrooms and Tougher Standards*. Houghton-Mifflin, Boston, MA.

[5] National Center on Health Statistics. U. S. Dept. of Health and Human Services, Presidential Bldg. 6525 Belcrest Rd, Hyattsville, MD. 20782.

[6] Mate, Gabor. 1999. *Scattered, How ADD Originates and What You Can Do about It*. E.P. Dutton.

[7] Kluger, Jeffrey and Alice Park. 2001. The quest for a Super Kid. *Time Magazine*, April 30, 2001. p. 53.

[8] Benson, Peter. 1999. All Kids Are Our Kids. President of the Search Institute in Minneapolis. Public Agenda Poll.

[9] DeGrandpre, Richard. 1999. *Ritalin Nation: Rapid-Fire Culture and the Transformation of Human Consciousness*. W. Norton, NY.

[10] Elkind, David. 1988. *The Hurried Child: Growing Up Too Fast Too Soon*. Reading, MA: Addison-Wesley Publishing Company; p. 4.

[11] Benson, Peter. 1997. *All Kids Are Our Kids, What communities must do to raise caring and responsible children and adolescents*. Jossey-Bass, San Francisco, CA. 314 p.

[12] McLean, Paul. Personal Communication.

[13] Messier, Paul, Barbara Given and Charlene Engel. 1994. National Learning Foundation Mission Statement. Presented in February 1994. National Learning Foundation, 11 Dupont Circle, N.W., Suite 900, Washington, DC 20036-1271.

[14] Seachrist, Lisa. 1995. Growing In and Out of Focus. In: *Science News*, Vol. 148. November 11, 1995. pp. 318-319.

[15] Wallis, Claudia. 1998. *Secrets to Academic Success*. In: *Time*, October 19, 1998.

[16] Michele Donley, Sheila Gribben, et. al. 1999. The Homework Ate My Family. *Time Magazine*: January 25, 1999 pp. 56 – 61.

[17] Dickinson, Amy. 1999. KinderGrind. Education Section, In: *Time*, November 8, 1999.

[18] Kirn, Walter and Wendy Cole. 2001. What Ever Happened to Play? In: *Time Magazine*, April 30, 2001. p. 56.

[19] Kohn, Alfe. 1998. *What To Look For In A Classroom And Other Essays*., Jossey-

Bass Pub. 1999. *Punished by Rewards: The Trouble With Gold Stars, Incentive Plans, A's, Praise, And Other Bribes.* Houghton Mifflin, NY.

[20] Morse, Jodie, Alice Park and James Willwerth. 1999. Troubled Kids. *Time: Special Report*: May 31, 1999, p. 34-49,

[21] Blackman, Ann, William Dowell, Margot Hornblower, et al. 1998 The Age of Ritalin. In: *Time*, November 30, 1998. pp. 84-94.

[22] DeGrandpre, Richard, 1999. p. 92

[23] Sept. 22, 1996. From What Teachers Check For. *Wisconsin State Journal*; 4G.

[24] IMS Health Canada

[25] DeGrandpre, Richard.

[26] Ibid. p. 200.

[27] Ibid.

[28] Blackman, Ann, et. al. 1998. *Time Magazine.*

[29] Ellison, Gaylord, 1993. Amphetamine, Cocaine: New brain link. Brain Research, January 1993. In: *Science News*, vol. 143, Jan. 16, 1992, p. 44.

[30] Rapaport, Judith L., et al. 1978. Dextriamphetamine; Cognitive and Behavioral Effects in Normal Prepubescent Boys. *Science*, Vol. 199, 560-63.

[31] DeGrandpre, Richard. p. 195.

[32] Ibid. p. 9

[33] Ibid. P. 181.

[34] Pollack, William. 1998. *Real Boys, Rescuing Our Sons from the Myths of Boyhood.* Henry Holt and Co., NY.

[35] Thompson, Michael and Dan Kindlon. 2000. *Raising Cain, the Emotional Life of Boys.* Ballantine Books, NY.

[36] Kraemer, Sebastian. 2001 Male Fragility. In. *British Medical Journal*

[37] Garbarino, James. 1999. *Lost Boys.* Anchor Books, NY.

[38] Mostofsky, Steward. 1999. ADD & ADHD. In: *Neuro News*, April 20, 1999.

[39] Matochik, John A. 1994. Brain images delve into hyperactivity. *American Journal of Psychiatry*. May 1994.

[40] McKearney, J. W. 1977. Asking Questions about Behavior. Perspectives. In: *Biology and Medicine*, 116.

[41] Diller, Lawrence. 1999. *Running On Ritalin, A Physician Reflects on Children, Society and Performance in a Pill.* Bantam, Doubleday and Dell Pub.

[42] Bailey, Becky. 1997. *There's Gotta Be A Better Way: Discipline That Works!.* Loving Guidance, Inc., P.O. Box 622407, Oviedo, FL. 32762. p. 129.

[43] Gibbs, Jeanne. 1995 *Tribes, A New Way of Learning and Being Together.* CenterSource Systems, LLC, 85 Liberty Ship Way, Suite 104, Sausalito, California 94965.

[44] Bohm, David. 1998. New Dimensions Radio, San Francisco, CA.

[45] Susan Kovalik and Associates, ITI Learning Model, 17051 SE. 272nd Str., Suite 17, Kent, Washington 98042. www.kovalik.com

[46] Bailey, Becky. 1997. pp. 165-180.

[47] Steiner, Rudolph. 1973. The Steinerbooks, Rudolph Steiner Publications. Blauvelt, NY.

[48] Bailey, Becky. 1997. pp.129-150.

[49] Fay, Jim, Foster W. Cline, and Bob Sornson. 2000. MEETING THE CHALLENGE, Using Love and Logic to help children develop attention and behavior skills. The Love and Logic Press Inc., Golden, Colorado, www.loveandlogic.com

Chapter 11: The Future of the Child Heart

[1] Kingsolver, Barbara. 1995. *High Tide in Tucson, Essays from now or never.* Harper Perennial, NY. pp. 99-107.

[2] White, Bowen. 1999. Why Normal Isn't Healthy. Touch the Future Conference, Monterey, Calif. Jan. 1999.

[3] Wegschneider-Cruze, Sharon. 1997. The Family Trap and *The Family Reconstruction: The Living Theater Model.* Science and Behavior Books.

[4] Vasconcellos, John. 1999. The First Person... The Time is Ripe: Are We? Touch the Future Conference, Monterey, CA. Jan., 1999.

[5] Maciocia, Giovanni.1994. *The Practice of Chinese Medicine.* Churchill Livingston Press, Edinburgh, London. pp. 198-202.

[6] The Yellow Emperor's Classic of Internal Medicine, Simple Questions (Huang Ti Nei Jing Su Wen), 1979 People's Health Pub. House, Beijing. First Pub. C. 100 BC., p. 58.

[7] *The Spiritual Axis (Ling Shu Jing),* People's Health Pub. House, Beijing, First Pub. C 100 BC, p. 128.

[8] Movie, The Way of the Dream.

[9] Bechara, Antoine, et. al. 1999. *Journal of Neuroscience,* July 1, 1999. In: *Science News,* vol. 156, p 59. July 24, 1999.

[10] Golman, Danial. 1995 *Emotional Intelligence.* Bantam Books, NY.

[11] Nowicki, S. and M. Duke. 1989. A measure of nonverbal processing ability in children between the ages of 6 and 10. Paper presented at the American Psychological Society meeting.

[12] Peters, Larry G. 1994. Rites of passage and the borderline syndrome: Perspectives in transpersonal anthropology. In: *ReVision,* Summer 94, Vol. 17(1), pp. 35-48.

[13] Ornish, Dean. 1998. *Love and Survival: 8 Pathways to Intimacy and Health.* Harper Collins, NY.

[14] Solamon, Paul. 1985. Audio Tape. Edgar Casey Foundation, Virginia Beach, VA.

[15] Turner, Rebecca, et. al. 1999. Psychiatry, Summer 1999. In: *Science News,* vol. 156, Aug 7, 1999. p. 90.

[16] Schwartz, Gary and Linda Russek. 1996. Science and Consciousness Conference. Tucson, AZ, March 1996.

[17] Ladinsky, Daniel. 1999. *The Gift, Poems By Hafiz, The Great Sufi Master.* Translations by Daniel Ladinsky. Penquin/Arkana, NY, NY.

[18] Dobson, Terry. 1985. *Aikido And The New Warrior.* Ed. By Richard Strozzi, North Atlantic Books, Berkeley, Calif. pp. 65-59.

L

M

N

O

P

R

S

Sufi 163
superconducting quantum interference device 41
supraliminal movement 77
survival 58, 59, 60, 61, 81, 113, 120, 121, 124, 130, 136, 154, 158
survival response 17, 28, 36
survival tactics 48
sympathetic nervous system 22, 50
systemic memory 82

T

Tae-gyo 100
Tai Chi 19, 52, 56
talking 30, 33, 96, 110
television 35, 79–80, 138, 145, 150
tendon guard reflex 22, 25
testing 143, 148
thalamus 49, 50, 122
thinking 53, 55, 133, 145, 158, 160
tickling 131, 133, 138
Tiller Modification 77
Tiller, William 42
touch 6, 32, 34, 36, 37, 41, 50, 56, 57–58, 64, 66, 98, 99, 102, 120, 123,
     126, 129–132, 130, 137–138, 151
Traditional Chinese Medicine 39, 55, 131, 159, 160
traditional Chinese teachings 31
Tribes 153
Truax, Barry 89
trust 2, 11–12, 37, 56, 132, 155, 158, 161, 163–164
trustworthy 158
TV 108, 109

U

Ubuntu 31
unified information field 76, 78, 81

V

Van Franz, Marie Louis 160
Vasconcellos, Senator John 158
vestibular system 72, 93, 95–96, 110, 111–113, 112, 115, 117, 124, 126
Vibrational Interference Patterns 43–46
vibrational spectrum 46
violence 32, 34, 68, 80, 136
violin 60, 89, 91, 103
VIP 41

vision 6, 9, 46, 72–74, 74, 76, 119, 130
visual memory 72

W

walk 16, 19, 21, 25, 56
Wennekes, Renate 125
Western culture 31
Western society 46, 151, 157, 160
White, David 110
Wolfe, Sidney 150

Y

yoga 16, 19, 52, 56

ABOUT THE AUTHOR

Carla Hannaford, Ph.D. is a biologist and educator with more than thirty years of teaching experience, including twenty years as a professor of biology and four years as a counselor for elementary and intermediate school children with learning difficulties.

Since 1988, she has been an internationally recognized educational consultant to twenty-seven countries. She was selected as a guest educator with the AHP-Soviet Project in 1988, has been recognized by Who's Who in American Education, and has received awards from the University of Hawaii and the American Association for the Advancements of Science for outstanding teaching in science.

She is the author of: *Smart Moves, Why Learning is Not All In Your Head,* published in 1995, which has sold over 100,000 copies in nine different languages, and *The Dominance Factor, How Knowing Your Dominant Eye, Ear, Brain, Hand & Foot Can Improve Your Learning,* published in 1997, which has sold over 75,000 copies in five different languages, both published by Great Ocean Publishers. She is also the author and co-producer of the Video *Education In Motion.*

She lives with her musician husband Ahti Mohala in Hawaii and Montana.

Carla and Breeze